D1270411

AFTER DIONYSUS

AFTER DIONYSUS:
An Essay on Where We Are Now

Henry Ebel

Rutherford • Madison • Teaneck
FAIRLEIGH DICKINSON UNIVERSITY PRESS

© 1972 by Associated University Presses, Inc.

Associated University Presses, Inc.
Cranbury, New Jersey 08512

Library of Congress Cataloging in Publication Data

Ebel, Henry, 1938–
  After Dionysus: an essay on where we are now.

  Bibliography: p.
  1. Apuleius Madaurensis. Metamorphoses.
2. Homerus. Ilias. I. Title.
            PA6217.E2   809   70-156321
                        ISBN 0-8386-7958-7
    Printed in the United States of America

NOTE

Portions of this book have appeared, though in substantially different form, in *Arion* (Department of Classics, University of Texas), *Arethusa* (Department of Classics, SUNY at Buffalo), and *College English.*

In the transliteration of Greek names, Greek and Latin forms have been mixed, the choice in each case being based on familiarity and the minimization of awkwardness.

Extracts from Jack Lindsay's translation of Apuleius, *The Golden Ass,* are reprinted by kind permission of Indiana University Press.

Extracts from Richard Lattimore's translation of Homer's *Iliad* are reprinted by kind permission of The University of Chicago Press.

Extracts from my "The Killing of Lykaon: Homer and Literary 'Structure'" are reprinted with permission of the National Council of Teachers of English; from my "Apuleius and the Present Time" with permission of *Arethusa;* and from my "A Better Tradition" with permission of *Arion.*

For
DALIA

CONTENTS

PREFACE

Of the humanities, what can survive? What deserves to survive? What *must* survive? And in what form? On what grounds?

The questions have been with us for years. They are obviously questions not only about our literature and art but about ourselves. How we relate to our past depends on what it is and what we are, and we can scarcely explore one of these considerations without beginning to learn something of the other.

This book has grown out of the conviction that our crisis is most sharply visible where we meet, or refuse to meet, our past, and that it is every bit as desperate as our most hyperbolic commentators imply, a universal agony of spirit and conviction.

"An old tradition," Paul Goodman rightly observes in his most recent book, "serves as a second line of defense to which alienated people can repair."[1] But before they can repair to it they have to have some idea of what it is. Goodman himself tends to see it as a repository of wisdom, virtue, heroism: old-fashioned ideals to stiffen a flabby or distracted present. The argument of this book is precisely the reverse: that our "old tradition," and

1. *The New Reformation* (New York: Random House, 1970), p. 109.

particularly classical literature, is of peculiar relevance to us because it is our mirror, not our antithesis.

In our sense of the absurd, our shift of interest from the written to the oral, our heightened consciousness of theater and role-playing, our struggle to find political roots beyond coercion and expediency, our yearning that the dialectic be ended and our fear that it is intensifying— in all of these ways we have steadily reclassicized ourselves. To read Homer or Virgil or Apuleius today is to be struck with a sense of nearly total relevance.

AFTER DIONYSUS

The bother with transmitting humane culture is that it must be re-created in spirit or it is a dead weight upon present spirit, and then it does produce timidity, pedantry, and hypocrisy. And then it is better forgotten.

—Paul Goodman

Like health or money, group identity presents no problem when it is an assured given, when the self-acceptance it generates is an unquestioned premise of life. It is only when it is failing to give a man an acceptable basis for pride in himself—or worse, forcing him into a pattern of self-rejection—that it becomes a problem and, sooner or later, a matter of crisis. This is precisely the point at which group identity and politics meet. It is the starting point of much notable history, of many notable lives.

—Harold R. Isaacs

1
APULEIUS
AND THE PRESENT TIME

i

Every age remakes its tradition, flashing the beam of its concerns over the corrugated surface of literary history. The freaks and sports of one age move to the center in the next; hallowed figures, whole hunks of time, recede to the shadows of academic interest. When the resurrection begins—of a Blake, or a Herman Hesse, or an Aubrey Beardsley—the successive moods are disbelief, condescension, ironic interest, and acceptance.

If we were to restructure our tradition at this very moment, Apuleius' *Metamorphoses* would probably achieve a position of relative importance. Twenty years ago such a development would have seemed inconceivable. We are ready to read Apuleius in a new way because, growing forward and backward, we are once again his contemporaries.

Whatever else he is, Apuleius isn't serious. Hence we can take him seriously. If there is anything we have gotten used to since the heyday of "maturity" and "serious-

13

ness" as literary values it is the idea of art as play and of the artist as a joyful tinkerer with the conventions and audiences available to him. Frank Kermode once spoke in the sixties of Shakespeare's "perversity," a sheer delight in complication and function, an unwillingness to merely accept or leave alone.

Outside of literature, too, we are reassessing our former distinctions between "playful" and "serious" art, and the conventional notion of a "serious" artist who has "playful" moments. The cumulative impact of Wölfflin, Giedion, and Gombrich has been to give us new eyes for baroque churches and rococo candlesticks and for the free and fantastic "making" that precedes—and can supplant—the tyranny of "matching."

In this way the age that has produced Joyce, Beckett, Borges, and Nabokov is reworking its past, repudiating, above all, the tyranny of "value" and "form" and the note of awed veneration that was felt, in the nineteenth century, to be suitable for discussions of Literature.

The relevance of Apuleius is obvious. In Book 9 of the *Metamorphoses*,[2] Lucius, the anti-hero who has been turned into an ass, overhears the story of a man who is hilariously cuckolded by his wife. Soon he is bought by a baker, and listens in while the baker's wife is told a tale of successful adultery by an old woman, "the confidante of her intrigues, and the bawd of her bitcheries" (Jack Lindsay's translation). Thus stimulated, the baker's wife prepares to commit adultery with the young man

---

2. For the *Metamorphoses* I have used the edition of D. S. Robertson and Paul Vallette, 3 vols. (Paris: Société d'édition "Les Belles Lettres," 1956). English translations used in the text are normally from the Jack Lindsay rendering, published under the title *The Golden Ass* (Bloomington, Ind.: Indiana University Press, 1967). Lindsay's titles for the Apuleian "tales" have been used as a convenience.

Philesitherus, who was the cuckolder of the old crone's story. The baker returns just as Philesitherus is being fed, and she hides her lover under a wooden bin. The first thing the baker does is to tell his wife a tale of adultery that mirrors his own situation: his friend the fuller has been cuckolded; he found his wife's lover under a wicker-cage in his house. With Lucius' help, it is a matter of moments before the baker discovers his own wife's lover.

This is one of many such complexes in the *Metamorphoses*. Together they give it an entirely playful, anti-realistic, absurdist texture, violating the Aristotelian canons of plot and form with gleeful persistence. Moreover, if form always implies exclusion—an artistic postponement of gratification—the *Metamorphoses* is distinguished by a kind of infinite inclusiveness. A French classicist describes the result: "Recueil d'histoires fabuleuses, roman érotique, symbole philosophique; oeuvre licencieuse, oeuvre satirique, oeuvre d'édification, les *Métamorphoses* ne sont rien de tout cela et sont tout cela en même temps."[3]

Total inclusiveness of this kind makes it less surprising, perhaps, that after Book 10 the work takes an abrupt turn toward total seriousness. Lucius is saved from his asinine condition by the intercession of Isis. He becomes a convert to her worship. Book 11, the closing section of the *Metamorphoses*, is a solemn description of religious experience.

But the conjuction of jokes and pornography with religious solemnity has always made students of Apuleius uncomfortable. One can see why. It is as if one of Sade's Gothic retreats had been invaded by a genuinely vir-

---

3. Robertson and Vallette, p. xxxv.

tuous archbishop seeking to redeem the souls of its
inhabitants. The anti-worlds of comedy and pornography
and romance have their own rules. One of them is the
inversion of whatever form of the reality principle a
society is most addicted to. In a society stressing ra-
tionality, trying to impose shape and predictability even
on its literature, Apuleius creates a triumphantly unpredictable universe in which the reader himself must
flounder about. But with the abrupt intrusion of Isis,
everything becomes predictable and ordered, even if the
ordering is theological rather than secular. The *Metamorphoses* seems to separate into discrete sections.

ii

For the medieval and Renaissance reader, what to us
seems a structural difficulty posed no problem at all.
Richard Adlington englished the *Metamorphoses* in 1566
and explained in his preface that he had initially been
attracted to Apuleius because he was funny. But then
Adlington came to believe that

> verily under the wrap of [Lucius's] transformation is taxed
> the life of mortal men, when as we suffer our minds so to
> be drowned in the sensual lusts of the flesh and the beastly
> pleasure thereof (which aptly may be called the violent
> confection of witches) that we lose wholly the use of reason
> and virtue, which properly should be in a man, and play the
> parts of brute and savage beasts. By like occasion we read
> [in the *Odyssey*] how divers of the companions of Ulysses
> were turned by the marvellous power of Circe into swine.[4]

4. Adlington's preface is reprinted in the Loeb Classical Library edition of Apuleius, ed. S. Gaselee (Cambridge, Mass.: Harvard University
Press, 1965), pp. xv–xviii.

A modern reader and critic like Professor Vallette sees the *Metamorphoses* at least partly as an erotic and pornographic novel: somehow these qualities coexist with philosophical and theological edification, including the attainment by the protagonist of a holy life and compulsory chastity. Adlington saw the sex, of course, but insisted that it was there only to be censured. The obvious objection, that Apuleius presents it in language too attractive to be disapproving, is (as we have gradually become aware in recent decades) less than overwhelming. The Renaissance inherited from the Middle Ages a real pleasure in giving sin its rhetorical innings, offering the reader a genuine and powerful temptation and therefore a greater and genuine triumph when sin is put down: the most famous examples are Satan's great oration to the fallen angels in *Paradise Lost* and Shylock's self-defense. Writers like C. S. Lewis and D. W. Robertson (to mention only those writing in English) have made a powerful case for an essential continuity between the classical and medieval worlds, so perhaps the same view of sin and rhetoric can be applied to the *Metamorphoses*.

In other words, can we escape Adlington at all? Only, I think, by expanding on his point, and understanding it as clearly as possible. We shy away from it because it seems to impose a deadeningly didactic—"typically medieval"—straitjacket on Apuleius, and to spoil our pleasure in the rollicking fun of his novel. We respond badly to an ethic that seems to put a disapproving limit on "self-realization," though we might be willing to admit that positive *obsession* is a bad thing.

But obsession is what the novel is about. Lucius informs us in the opening section that he was "always thirsty for every sip of novelty." In the book's first tale within a tale, the merchant Socrates meets disaster when he abandons his business itinerary and rushes off on a detour to see some widely publicized gladiatorial games. The Latin here carries resonances missing in Lindsay's translation, for it introduces the crucial Apuleian concept of voluptas or passionate gratification, a libidinal energy that cannot be suppressed: his troubles began, Socrates declares, "dum voluptatem gladiatorii spectaculi satis famigerabilis consector." The point is driven home again at the very beginning of Book 2, where Lucius declares that "I am normally eager and only too inclined to ferret out the Rare and the Marvellous."

The point that Apuleius is making is identical with that of D. H. Lawrence: that there is such a thing as self-realization and that we very seldom, if ever, see it in the people around us or in ourselves. The craving is there in the depths of our being, but in the process of trying to satisfy itself it becomes diverted into trivial, feverish, and obsessive behavior. Like the odious cosmopolites from whom the Lawrencian hero (or more commonly, heroine) is trying to escape, Apuleius' average men are restless, gossipy, promiscuous, endlessly stimulated, and endlessly bored. Lawrence's categories are close to the Paulinian or early Christian understanding of the spiritual dialectic: to let go is to find, to die is to live, to live without God (on a merely conscious and willful level) is to die. Apuleius, writing a century or so after Paul, makes it clear that a dialectical understanding of this kind was widely diffused in the society of the Empire.

The feverish quest of Lucius and his contemporaries, thought it may look superficially like a broadening of self and experience, is actually the very opposite. Ranging ever more widely, they leave themselves further behind. As in Kafka, the world becomes a terrible maze; thrashing about for relief, the psyche implicates itself more and more deeply; the rhythm of things moves toward an overwhelming crisis.

At this point we can return to Adlington, who, once he has explained his general interpretation of what Apuleius is getting at, concludes his preface with a burst of what Matthew Arnold used to describe as the quaint and fantastic conceits of the Middle Ages:

> But as Lucius Apuleius was changed into his human shape by a rose, the companions of Ulysses by great intercession, and Nebuchadnezzar by the continual prayers of Daniel, whereby they knew themselves and lived after a good and virtuous life: so can we never be restored to the right figure of ourselves, except we taste and eat the sweet rose of reason and virtue, which the rather by mediation of prayer we may assuredly attain.[5]

We are likely to balk at reason and virtue—distressingly medieval virtues—but the rest of what Adlington has to say has a surprisingly contemporary ring. Cedric Whitman uses almost identical language in his book *Homer and the Heroic Tradition* as he tries to explain what the *Odyssey* is all about. Odysseus is a man who "defines, rather than discovers, himself, each experience involving, and at last dissipating, a particular shade of that anonymity which overhangs a man until his context is complete." And Whitman comments on the strata of myth underlying the *Odyssey* that "the nature of myth, or folk tale, is to reflect in external form the psyche's subconscious exploration of itself and its experience."[6]

---

5. *Ibid.*
6. *Homer and the Heroic Tradition* (Cambridge, Mass.: Harvard University Press, 1958), pp. 297–98.

The *Metamorphoses*, of course, are very close to the *Odyssey*. Like Petronius, Apuleius is partly engaged in satirizing Homeric and Virgilian heroics. Poseidon in the *Odyssey*, Juno in the *Aeneid*, Priapus in the *Satyricon*, and Fortuna in the *Metamorphoses* are divinities who come to connote a primary malevolent or chaotic energy in the universe, what we ourselves call entropy, what Freud ultimately designated as Thanatos, what the Middle Ages and Renaissance projected into the figure of Satan. And the issue of sex is always close to the surface because orgasm represents a kind of crucial organic concession to the force that would otherwise overwhelm us; as, on a broader scale, do the "dying god," and the archetypal hero's descent into and escape from the underworld.

In other words, Homer and Apuleius saw with exceptional conscious clarity and sympathy a recurrent pattern in folk-tale and myth, and each was able to draw these stories into a larger schema that joins the eternal and archetypal with the realistic and particular. Apuleius had the additional advantage of being able to use both the corpus of folk-tale that was "native" to him *and* the comparable materials that had already found their way into the works of his predecessors. His position resembles that of Shakespeare, who also wove together indigenous folk-tale, general classical mythology, and literary sources.

The specifically Christian categories of Adlington's interpretation can thus be seen, like the Christian myth itself, as the subtype of a general and pervasive concern in human story-making, which in turn reflects the most crucial dilemmas of man's life in a universe from which he is separate, but of which he is, nevertheless, mysteriously a part.

iii

All of this suggests that Adlington is correct when he treats the *Metamorphoses* as fundamentally a unity. At the same time one must admit that medieval interpreters, drawing on Augustinian notions, were able to extract unified "deeper meanings" from some very unpromising materials. And there does hang over some of his remarks the fantastic quality of which medieval exegesis was capable, so that the rose that Lucius nibbles to free himself from his donkeyhood becomes "the sweet rose of reason and virtue." Similarly, we are unlikely to accept the ruthless allegorism of Thomas Taylor, who saw the *Metamorphoses* (in 1795) as a precise transcription of Platonic ideas.

Our own critical bias—a good one—is to postpone judgment about the ideational content of a work until we sense that the ideas are structurally operative. Can we validate the unity of the *Metamorphoses* on structural grounds?

But there is scarcely a slipperier word in the vocabulary of literary criticism than "structure," with its spatial and architectural connotations. Particularly is this the case when we are discussing a work pervaded with motifs that recur insistently in almost every episode, tale, and chapter: the motifs (to name only the most important) of Fortuna and vicissitude, of metamorphosis, of restless curiosity, of death and resurrection, of magic, and of true or false religion. Since the motifs, though they can be separated out into "strands" and no doubt statistically tabled, are powerfully complementary, the resulting impression on the reader as he makes his way through the book is better described in musical or electronic than in architectural terms. Whereas a structural analogy continually encourages us to ask what the paraphrasable function or purpose of a motif is—why it occurs at *that* precise point in the "construction" of the work—music provides us with an analogical language in which repetitions and variations *are* the structure, which welds recognition and response, and which shares with literature the indispensable fact of being experienced in *time*. Indeed, the temptation is to apply wholesale to the *Metamorphoses* the approach that Northrop Frye takes to Shakespearean romance:

> The only place where the tradition of Shakespearean romantic comedy has survived with any theatrical success is, as we should expect, in opera. . . . The operatic features of Shakespearean comedy are an integral part of Shakespeare's concentration on the theatrical process. Thematic images and words echo and call and respond in a way which is a constant fascination to anyone working with the text. Such repetitions seem to have something oracular about them, as though arranging them in the right way would provide a key to some occult and profound process of thought.[7]

Frye's use of "seem" encapsulates his argument. He accepts Coleridge's dictum that all literary critics are either *Iliad* or *Odyssey* critics; extends this observation to a distinction between tragedy on the one hand and comedy and romance on the other; and concludes that whereas tragedy is ineluctably related to reality—attracts its critics because it seems to offer "a deeper understanding of the nonliterary center of experience"—comedy and romance tend (in words that Frye applies specifically to Shakespeare) to draw us "away from the analogy to

7. *A Natural Perspective* (New York: Harcourt, Brace and World, 1965), p. 25.

familiar experience into a strange but consistent and self-contained dramatic world." Comedy and romance are marked, in other words, by patterns of conscious stylization that can only be justified in antirealistic or arealistic terms and that thus run counter to the predominant critical tendency of modern times: the defense of literature as an illumination of human reality.

Frye's description of romance is 1) highly pertinent to Apuleius, because it captures an essential quality of his method, and 2) the most coherent evidence to date for the removal of Apuleius from the "romance" category. For although the characteristic operations of the *Metamorphoses* are musical and repetitive, there is no question that Apuleius' repetitions *do* have "something oracular about them": that they are intended to prefigure, anticipate, and reinforce the great leap of spirit and sensibility with which the book concludes. For example, all the lesser resurrections in the novel, some silly, some fraudulent, some the result of gross magic, converge on the spiritual death and rebirth of Book 11, where the priest says of the worship of Isis: "the act of initiation [has] been compared to a voluntary death with a slight chance of redemption." All the vicissitudes and reversals in the book, some comic, some deadly, acquire a new meaning when Lucius turns to the Great Goddess and pleads, in the classic language of conversion:

> Support my broken life, and give me rest and peace after the tribulations of my lot. Let there be an end to the toils that weary me, and an end to the snares that beset me.[8]

But if we remove Apuleius from the category of "romance," at least as so usefully defined by Frye, where

---

8. Lindsay translation, p. 236.

are we to put him? And if we can find a better category for him, who else and what else will be in it?

What we are groping toward is a category that will transcend the very distinctions Frye so brilliantly makes, one that will enable us to articulate clearly the conjunction of seriousness and playfulness that Apuleius attains.

iv

Later in this book I will argue that the *Iliad,* that fountainhead of "great tragedy," has some distinctly "Apuleian" qualities. It too is structured in such a way as to call the very term "structure" into question; even more than the *Metamorphoses,* its texture consists of prefiguring, echo, and analogy on a scale so broad and so intense as to reach the outer margins of credibility.

But our instinctive revulsion at a comparison of Apuleius and Homer is likely to have thematic rather than structural grounds. It stems from the Arnoldian (and characteristically nineteenth-century) idea that there is a quality called "high seriousness" and that the works containing it can be clearly delimited from those that are merely amusing.

A reading of *Hamlet* sans incense should be enough to indicate that amusement and profundity can stand in a complementary rather than antithetical relationship. Homer's fun, like Hamlet's, is savage. Can one really not laugh when the wrathful Achilles sends Patroclus into battle and counsels him to self-restraint? The laughter thus forced from us deepens rather than negates the climactic moment in Book 16 that so much of the poem anticipates by gnomic prophecy and analogy: the killing of Patroclus. If Apuleius cannot quite be described as a savage ironist, neither is he genial except to those who read him (as they once read Chaucer) with genial eyes. The funniest sentence in the *Metamorphoses* is the first, where Apuleius described himself as the teller of a mere Milesian tale; even funnier are those who believe him.

What we have to make allowance for is a category of work that has the autonomous, clockwork quality Frye assigns to comedy and romance and that is nevertheless "saying something"—and something of immense power—about human reality. The clockwork is wondrous to behold, but the gears, levers, and springs have been carefully selected: the intertwining and echoing motifs are those of death and life, identity and annihilation, humanity and the universe—the binding and perennial concerns of our species. In this category I would unhesitatingly place not only Homer and Apuleius (and Virgil and Dante) but much of Shakespeare: the author, at any rate, of all those plays that consciously and overtly play with their own illusionism—with the theater as reality and reality as a theater—in order to play *upon* the audience. Frye is fascinatingly mistaken when he amalgamates all of Shakespeare to what he sees as the autonomous structuralism of comedy and romance and declares "that Shakespeare had no opinions, no values, no philosophy, no principles of anything except dramatic structure." Nothing could be truer than that Shakespeare is of a piece and that no firm line divides the tragedies, comedies, and romances. No one could be on a falser track than the critic who scours the plays for "values" in the sense of an Elizabethan World Picture to which Shakespeare regularly pledged allegiance. But drama, as Shakepeare supremely realized (and enables us to realize), *is* a value. The alternative reality it presents us with, and the way in which that reality works on us, pinpoints the philosophical problem of human perception and understanding: the "uncertainty principle" that is built into our relations with the world around us, the artificiality (and therefore the malleability) of the structures of understanding that enable us to locate ourselves in the universe and therefore to function.

What is true of drama is true of all literature. It is simply that drama intensifies the truth by visibly segregating its alternative reality on a stage or within a magic circle. Once we have rid ourselves of the unspeakable limitations our culture has placed on the verb *to play*, we will have little difficulty in acknowledging that the most playful literature is also the most profound. Metamorphosis is not just a "theme" in literature; it is what literature is all about. One cannot compose a fiction without creating an alternative reality and one cannot create an alternative reality without dislocating the "reality" that we insist, in our more reflective moments, is the "true" one. All authors, even the humblest, are therefore concerned with metamorphosis. Those who have dealt with it (or played with it) more explicitly have been those great enough to reflect on their capacities and to integrate their reflections into the very process of creation. One could hardly ask for more.

v

To revalue an author means, among other things, to stop taking him, or anything about him, for granted. It would be a tedious exercise to collect from historians the capsule paragraphs on Apuleius whose hidden or explicit assumption is that he represents (unconsciously, of course) a stage in the development of his society: for example, that Apuleius' "belief" in magic demonstrates the persistence or growth of irrationalism within a world whose dominant modes of organization were pragmatic and secular.

In truth, of course, Apuleius' achievement is not that he enables us to diagnose his society but that he does it himself. We cannot know what aspects of himself, or of himself before conversion, Apuleius "put into" Lucius. We can be quite certain that Lucius—restless, curious, endlessly eager for novelty and excitement—is intended to be a representative of the general humanity of his time. Apuleius' portrait of the social and political realities of the Roman world is similarly precise. In the introduction to his translation of the *Metamorphoses,* Jack Lindsay glances at "the general crisis of the third century" that "finally issued in the Constantinean State" and then observes that "Apuleius, needless to say, is no political prophet who foresees the coming crisis; but he is a great and sensitive artist who feels the subterranean tremors in the human sphere." Lindsay's antithesis between prophecy and impressionism seems to me to fall left and right of the target. Apuleius' presentation of the crisis of spirit in his world is carried beyond mere feeling by its unmistakable diagnostic fullness. And the question worth asking is not whether Apuleius' analysis "prophesies" the crisis of the third century—what possible *literary* relevance can such a question have?—but what it leads to within the work itself.

Once we begin to discuss the *Metamorphoses* as a conscious, created, and perhaps even adequate fiction, the work comes crisply into focus, its levels and concerns profoundly complementary. The personal psychology of Lucius, the instability of a world where the defense of private property suffuses mankind with hatred and distrust, the development of many Luciuses in tropistic adaptation to the world they must inhabit, the universal fact (of which "magic" is as much an expression as a cause) that all appearances are unreliable and all "realities" transient, the unexpected twists and turns of a plot whose movement exemplifies the nature of what it portrays—everything that looks eccentric or of mere historical interest when taken separately turns out to fit a larger picture of intense and intrinsic significance.

The pivot upon which all this turns in the *Metamorphoses* is clearly to be sought in the references to Fortuna. These references are so continual, and the conversion in Book 11 is so explicitly declared to be a release from Fortuna's vicissitudes, that the book might be criticized as an especially heavy-handed application of a theme that "occupies an important place in antique literature and that antique philosophical ethics often takes . . . as a starting point."[9] That this is not the case is because Apuleius' conception of Fortuna differs from the common Roman vision of the goddess as bestower and withdrawer of the good luck that accrues to individuals, and achieves what can only be called a philosophical breadth.

This is not to say that the traditional view is absent from the book: Lucius often speaks of Fortuna's cruelty or animosity as a sufficient explanation of the torments he undergoes, and in these references Fortuna has the role of Poseidon in the *Odyssey* and Priapus in the

---

9. Erich Auerbach, *Mimesis* (New York: Doubleday Anchor Books, 1957), p. 24.

Satyricon.[10] But the progress of the narrative, with its
pervasive emphasis on vicissitude, mutability, paradox,
and reversal lends particular weight to those more con-
certed passages in which the direct malice of an anthro-
pomorphized divinity gives way instead to the portrait
of a randomized and absurd universe. Early in the book
a character explains his catastrophic experiences by attributing them to "the sliddery twists, the freakish whirli-
gigs, the ceaseless vicissitudes of Fortune" (*Fortunarum
lubricas ambages et instabiles incursiones, et reciprocas
vicissitudines*). The language here and elsewhere in the
Metamorphoses shifts our attention from personalized
divinity to world-pervading process, and from the personal fate of Lucius (which can easily be read as divine
malice or chastisement) to the pattern—or dispatterning—
of the *Metamorphoses* as a whole. In Book VII, Lucius
reflects

> that not without due cause did the antique philosophers
> insist on describing Fortune as stone-blind, with eyes un-
> socketed. For she invariably confers her riches on the base
> and undeserving, and never once favours a mortal whom
> she could respect. Always she attaches herself to men whom
> if she could see she would forsake instantly.[11]

Irrational hostility can be part of a rationally ordered
universe: once its source is perceived it is predictable.

---

10. In our own terms, of course, this is an "inconsistency," and
Apuleius' inconsistencies (like Homer's) have attracted a good deal
of attention. Our enhanced understanding of the oral/rhetorical tradition has considerably reduced the significance of this kind of discrep-
ancy. But our groping after metaphors indicates the difficulty we still
have in describing a mode of composition loose enough to accom-
modate clear discrepancies and yet more highly "structured," in the
complexity of its repetitive and intertwining motifs, than our own literature of the past three centuries.
11. Lindsay translation, p. 149.

But the world that is ruled by a blind goddess who cannot even please herself might as well be governed by a dead one. What has snapped here is the last fragile cord of rationalization that enables a man amid catastrophe (or sects like the Gnostics and Manichaeans) to speak of a hostile universe. What Apuleius is telling us is that the mundane universe intends nothing at all.

Apuleius' vision of an absurd universe meshes perfectly with the twin themes of the *Metamorphoses*: the complete unreliability of appearances, and the resulting ease of transformation of one deceptive solid into another. This applies not only to those magical episodes in which a woman becomes a bird or an old man a dragon, but to those moments when a solid and well-founded opinion about another human being—that he is a friend, or hospitable, or selfless, or an enemy—turns out to be the diametrical opposite of the truth. The blindness of Fortuna is mirrored by the blindness of men who bump about acting on mistaken hypotheses, which in turn are governed by the utter unreliability of appearances. And the reader is himself drawn into the process each time he is "surprised" by the twists, turns, and paradoxes of the narrative: when, for example, the decrepit old woman of Book 6, who is addressed by one of the robbers she keeps house for as "you creaking old corpse . . . too dirty to be alive, and . . . not enough go in you to fall dead," produces the exquisite tale of Cupid and Psyche.

The synoptic effect of all this reminds one of Joyce's aphorism that "history is a nightmare from which I am trying to awaken." The dreamlike atmosphere of the *Metamorphoses* has often been commented on, but with the conventional suggestion that "dream" is an antonym for "reality." In fact, as all modern psychological theory has tended to emphasize, our confidence in a rational and predictable universe is exceedingly fragile, and dependent on continual artificial reinforcement (or reassurance) from our society. Dream or nightmare, in which our struggles to act merely enmesh us deeper in the condition of *being acted upon*, tell the true story that we manage to conceal from ourselves in our waking hours.

Joyce was talking about the twentieth century, a time when the pressure of "outside events" has tended increasingly to disjoin or ironize the daily, domestic stabilities of human life. Partly, of course, this has been the result of direct disruption; but the vicarious experience of catastrophe, or the unending *anticipation* of disaster, has been of much greater significance in steadily widening the gap between our surface and inner lives. Thus, our reaction to a dystopia like that portrayed in *Nineteen Eighty-Four* is often one of recognition rather than shocked horror, like a Kafka character accepting a grotesque but obviously inescapable destiny.

Like Orwell, like Kafka, like Freud, Apuleius forces our dreams upon us during the hours when we are normally able to avoid them: Lucius and Gregor Samsa, ass and bug, are ways of riveting us to the panic undertone of our lives. To live in a world ruled by Fortuna is to experience *The Castle*. The dreamlike conjunction of hilarity and horror in the *Metamorphoses,* in which death becomes a joke and jokes end in death, is what we encounter again and again in modern literature.

Apuleius makes us keenly aware, in other words, that our own complex of feeling about humanity and the universe has occurred before, at specific and critical moments in human history. Late antiquity was one such time, the Renaissance another; hence the obvious appeal of Apuleius' ideas to the world that produced LeRoy's *De la vicissitude*, Spenser's Mutability Cantos, and the incomparable meditation on appearance and reality that we find in *A Midsummer-Night's Dream*. To pinpoint Apuleius' relevance to our own time, here are some acute remarks on Saul Bellow by Jack Richardson:

> If there is a notion of fate in Bellow's works, it is that good men are destined, and know it, to misconceive life again and again. Throughout the book, Herzog chases continually a reality which refuses to bow to the preconceptions formed of it by an imaginative intelligence. At one instant life seems a madman's dream, but no sooner has one armed oneself against this flamboyant guise than it changes into something small and ordinary. . . . This sense of the antic perversity of life, its refusal to live up to the simplest or most elaborate human expectation, pervades almost all of Bellow's work.[12]

There is some truth in the McLuhanesque notion that we have reprimitivized ourselves. The genius of classical literature was to carry into a new age and new forms the primitive sense of a permeable and dangerous universe through which man makes his perilous way: a cosmic theater in which everything is aware of human destinies except the human victim himself, blundering inexorably toward his doom. The presence of comparable ideas in Renaissance and modern literature hardly needs documenting. A century of revisionist anthropology has made us fully aware, by now, that this primitive vision is in fact the most sophisticated one available to us, that by adopting the Cartesian framework of modern rationalism

---

12. In the *New York Review of Books* for March 13, 1969.

Europeans paid a heavy philosophical and cultural price.

But this simultaneous primitivization and sophistication is more than a matter of philosophy: it deeply involves questions of literary style and structure, the communication of a "point" through the very texture of a narrative. Here too Apuleius is accessible to us, for here too we have become Apuleian in our sensibilities.

2
PARATAXIS AND
MONTAGE

i

The typical style of the *Metamorphoses* is musical and repetitive. There is hardly anything in the book that doesn't have its analogy in another section; the resulting swirl of motifs is like a cloud of insects on a summer's day. But the insects are identical (at least to *our* eyes) and therefore anonymous, and the Apuleian motifs are individual and carefully chosen. To the dreamlike, almost hypnotic, effect of repetitive motion must be added a series of intensifying recognitions that anticipate the climactic revelation of Book 11. If the *general* movement of the *Metamorphoses* is precisely an apotheosis of movement and process that would resist "spatial" diagramming, its recurrent particulars give it what we cannot help but call "shape" and "form."

The crucial question is how the two elements, temporal succession and spatial shape, are joined together. Merely to say that one is "added" to the other would beg the essential question of how they are *experienced* by the reader, and would leave untouched the most remarkable aspect of Apuleian (and classical) literary intelligence, the communication-through-disjunction that we might call either parataxis or montage.

ii

The dominating form of the *Metamorphoses* is a downward and upward curve, a symbolic death and resurrection, that connects the successive adventures and tales of the book. The downward curve begins with the book itself and reaches its nadir in Book 8, in the Tale of the Bailiff;[13] the upward curve begins almost immediately thereafter and culminates in what can be described, with more justice than usual, as the "high point" of the work: a religious conversion that takes place in spring, amid all the signs of a general rebirth.

The curve consists of the first decreasingly and then increasingly modified ghastliness of the adventures and tales themselves. Since "ghastliness" may look like an inordinately subjective category, it is worth quoting the Tale of the Bailiff in full, particularly since its brevity is significantly related to the functional role it plays in the book:

> There was once a servant who was entrusted by his master with full control of the estate, and who acted as bailiff for the extensive farming-property where we were putting-up. This man had married one of his fellow-servants; but he fell into guilty intercourse with a free-woman of the outer world. Griped with rage at discovery of this pecca-

13. Lindsay translation, p. 178.

dillo, his wife burned all his account books and everything that she could collect out of his storeroom. Then, not satisfied with this retaliation upon her erring bedmate, she turned her wrath back upon her own bowels, twisted a rope round her neck, tied it to a baby which she had borne her husband, and jumped into a deep well, baby and all.

The master was extremely annoyed at her death, and ordered the arrest of a servant who had provoked his wife to such unseemly conduct. Then he had the man stripped, smeared all over with honey, and bound fast to a fig-tree, where a countless horde of ants (hurrying trickles of quick-life) had built their nests in the rotten trunk.

As soon as the ants smelt the honey sweating out of the man's body, they swarmed upon him; and with tiny multitudinous nips they shred by shred pincered out all his flesh and entrails. The man hung on this cross of slow torture till he was picked quite clean; and the skeleton can be seen to this very day strung up on the tree of death, dry white bones.

One ought to note first of all that the tale doesn't violate the general practice of the *Metamorphoses*, but is joined to the book as a whole by analogy and echo. The relationship of the adulterous bailiff and his murderous wife is *anticipated* in the relationship of Milo and the adulterous Pamphile (Book 3) and of the adulterously inclined sisters in the Tale of Cupid and Psyche (Books 4, 5, and 6), while antitheses are provided by the selfless marriages of Cupid and Psyche and Charite and Tlepolemus (Books 7 and 8). It is *echoed* by the complex of adulteries we have already noted at the baker's mill (Book 9). The sadism with which the bailiff is killed has its own anticipations and echoes: until we reach Book 11 human cruelty seems inseparable from humanity, with the most bloodcurdling threats and acts occurring in proximity to the Tale of the Bailiff itself.

Having acknowledged these ties to the rest of the book, one must end by saying that in every other way the Tale of the Bailiff stands alone. For one thing, it is not a tale at all but a synopsis of catastrophe, brief, relentless, and mechanical. If the narrative paradigm of the *Metamorphoses* is the unexpected or inexplicable turn of plot, the revelation of universal vicissitude through the flux of events, then this tale is distinguished by the remorseless linear certainty with which its events succeed each other.

The Tale of the Bailiff is flanked by two episodes that complement its vision of horror. It is immediately preceded by the pilgrimage of disaster that begins with the suicide of Charite and is Apuleius' most sustained presentation of the hopeless and even fatal unreliability of "what seems to be true." The travelers are first mistaken for robbers and ferociously mauled by dogs and villagers. They bind their wounds in a pastoral grove that is in fact (as a passing goatherd indicates) a place of death. And the meaning of this becomes clear when they take pity on a weeping old man who pleads with them to save his little grandson, only to lead the young man who volunteers into the jaws of a monstrous dragon.

The Tale of the Bailiff is immediately followed by an abyss of a different kind. Lucius is purchased by the ghastly homosexual priests, "charlatans that turn the Syrian Goddess into a beggar-wench, huckstering her about the highways and the towns, and jingling on cymbals and castanets." If the pilgrimage of disaster represents the ultimate concentrated negation of all appearances, and the Tale of the Bailiff a similarly compressed negation of all human virtue, mercy, and relationship, the priests of the Syrian Goddess (who are notably successful in their swindling until they commit a foolish and

unnecessary theft) represent the radical antithesis of all
religion, the point in the *Metamorphoses* at which we are
furthest from Isis. The three episodes stand fittingly
together at the very nadir of the work.[14]

If we take the Tale of the Bailiff as a starting point
and move from it both forward and backward in the
book, what will strike us, I think, is that as we approach
the "extremities"—the beginning and the end—the overriding pattern of vicissitude remains but is increasingly
admixed with a measure of redeeming virtue or goodness.
The gang of robbers who steal Lucius almost as soon as
he has been transformed into an ass can scarcely be called
romantic figures—we should note the drooling sadism of
the punishment they concoct for Lucius and Charite at
the end of Book 6—yet they are almost unique within
the *Metamorphoses* in achieving a heroism that echoes
Homer and Virgil. (The apparent exception actually con-
firms the point: the three heroic brothers in Book 9
"echo" or "balance" the robbers in hysteron-proteron
fashion, and as is appropriate in the book's "rising" curve
their heroism has no element of satire.) The heroic
thief Lamachus first surrendered his arm and then

> drew his sword with his left hand; and after kissing the
> blade repeatedly he thrust it with determined force deep
> into his breast. . . . Thus he found an end worthy the hero-
> ism of his life.[15]

The satire here is obvious but in Apuleius as in Petronius
satire does not cancel out its narrative vehicle. Apuleius
is satirizing his thieves but also the world of the Empire,

14. The tripartite division is typically Apuleian. See Paul Junghanns,
Die Erzählungstechnik von Apuleius' Metamorphosen und Ihrer Vorlage
(Leipzig: Dieterich'sche Verlagsbuchhandlung, 1932).

15. Lindsay translation, p. 94.

whose exclusive concern with private property and its security—the very basis of the Augustan settlement—confines heroic self-sacrifice and most other virtues to its outcasts.

If we move from the Tale of the Bailiff toward the end of Book 9 we find Lucius in the home of a poor farmer, living in circumstances almost as dreadful as those of the baker's mill earlier in the same book. But the starvation and misery have become fraternal, "for both my master and myself had meals equal in size and substance." The sharing of goods here echoes the examples of selflessness earlier in the *Metamorphoses* and anticipates the more desirable human conditions that the ass comes to share in Book 10: first as the property of two brothers (by whom "I was . . . received as a kind of third brother") and then as the boon companion of the wealthy Thiasus.

To radiate the *Metamorphoses* outward and upward from the Tale of the Bailiff is to imply that the work may be organized, however approximately and assymetrically, in that most available of ancient literary forms, the hysteron proteron. Such a pattern does seem to be at work both at the center and at the extremities of the work (the section in between, which includes the Tale of Cupid and Psyche, will be discussed in a moment). The conversion in Book 11 is clearly the corresponding "answer" to the state of mind repeatedly presented to us in the opening pages of the *Metamorphoses*—the lust for novelty, the restlessness, and the thrill-seeking. If we move inward another step from the extremities we arrive at the sexuality that is so significant a part of the *Metamorphoses* and that has been, since the eighteenth century, persistently misunderstood.

In Books 1, 2, and 3, and in Book 10, Lucius finds
himself the guest of a wealthy man. As the human guest
of the niggardly Milo he is treated rather worse than a
donkey; as the beloved ass of Thiasus he achieves a
luxury any human might envy. In a corresponding paral-
lelism, the sexual combats of Lucius and Fotis in Books
2 and 3 have their echo in the sexual involvements of
Lucius the ass. The connection will seem absurd only
to those who read Books 2 and 3 under the aegis of the
Playboy philosophy, and perfectly appropriate when we
note Erich Auerbach's comment in *Mimesis* on Apuleius'

> predilection for a haunting and gruesome distortion of re-
> ality. I have in mind not only the numerous metamorphoses
> and ghost stories . . . but also many other things—the quality
> of the eroticism, for instance. With an extreme emphasis
> on desire, which all the spices of rhetorico-realistic art are
> employed to arouse in the reader too, there is a complete
> absence of human warmth and intimacy. There is always
> an admixture of something spectrally sadistic; desire is
> mixed with fear and horror; though to be sure there is a
> good deal of silliness too.[16]

Auerbach has identified the central function and operation in Apuleius of what in another writer might be simple
pornography. Pornography is unique in literature for its
utilitarian self-containment. The sexual arousal of the
reader is simultaneously means and end. The pornographic writing in Apuleius at first looks very similar:
fully developed, intentional, artfully deployed, and qualified only by its own hypertrophy—that is, by what Auerbach himself admits to be highly implicit, a "quality"
that is ultimately an "absence." But if we go beyond
Auerbach's impressionism we will find the pornographic

---

16. Auerbach, pp. 52–53.

sections of the *Metamorphoses* qualified and "placed" by a mode of composition that could be called structural parataxis, the placing side by side, not (in the accepted meaning of *parataxis*) of clauses, phrases, and words, but of episodes and scenes.

We can see Apuleius' use of the technique with particular clarity in the latter part of Book 10. Here the sequence of events is as follows:

1. The love-making of Lucius the ass with "a rich and respected lady."

2. The Tale of the Jealous Wife, giving the history of the condemned murderess with whom Lucius is to mate in the arena.

3. The "first act" in the arena: i.e., the masque of the Judgment of Paris.

4. The preparations for the public copulation of the murderess and the ass, and the escape of Lucius.

The movement through these four episodes encapsulates the dialectical narrative technique of the *Metamorphoses*. The first is itself a reversal of the increasingly good fortune Lucius has enjoyed: he is betrayed to the lustful lady by a corrupt servant, the first act of dishonesty he has encountered since the recognition of his humanoid talents. But the experience proves unexpectedly pleasurable, so much so that not only Adlington but even Jack Lindsay has felt it necessary to expurgate his translation. The love-making exactly fits Auerbach's characterization of Apuleius as a master of the pornographic-grotesque.

This double reversal is tripled when Lucius' benefactor Thiasus, having learned of the ass's amorous capacities, abruptly becomes his tormentor by deciding to have him copulate in public. (At the very end of Book 10 he personally superintends the preparation of the nuptial couch for Lucius and the murderess.) And the decision is followed by the terrible Tale of the Jealous Wife, a story of unremitting murderousness that recalls —and is meant to recall—the Tale of the Bailiff, being set off from the latter not by any absence of horrors but by the crucial fact that the catastrophe grows out of great goodness rather than betrayal: a mother who loves her child and wants to save it from death (compare the Bailiff's wife, who kills her infant with herself), a young man who is a model of affection and duty. The story, whose sheer grisliness is impossible to paraphrase, is instantly followed by a lyrical description of the return of spring and the exquisite masque of the Judgment of Paris, whose centerpriece is the appearance of a girl impersonating Venus:

> but Venus when a virgin. She was rather unclad, and the grace that her nakedness uttered had no flaw. Unclad she was, save for a gauzy silken scarf which shadowed her admirable loins, and which sometimes lifted at the gay twitch of the lascivious wind to show how truly young she was, and sometimes clung the closer to delineate more deliciously the moving contours of her body.[17]

This is pornography of a different order, unmixed with travesty, obsession, or bestiality. The Venus of the masque —it is typical of Apuleius that a mere actress should so successfully incarnate what she only "appears to be"— is fittingly described a few lines later as "dominae voluptatum," the Queen of Voluptas, in Lindsay's inevitable

---

17. Lindsay translation, p. 231.

but inadequate translation "the Queen of Pleasure." But Voluptas is as central in the *Metamorphoses* as Fortuna. The closing sentence of the Tale of Cupid and Psyche tells us that Psyche, after her marriage, bore Cupid a daughter named Voluptas, and at this point Lindsay translates the word as Joy. Clearly he is wrestling with the English language, which so remorselessly classifies the qualities of life into those which are essentially physical and those which are essentially mental. But Voluptas, in its potent onomatopoeia, connotes a "pleasure principle" that cuts across and transcends these categories, an intensity of gratification that welds mind and body and subordinates neither.

We find Voluptas in pure form in the relationship of Cupid and Psyche, in the subsequent love affair of Charite and Tlepolemus, and (allowing for the play on "appearances") in the masque of the Judgment of Paris. But the life-giving and positive erotic force it connotes has ultimate and perhaps tragic limits. Psyche's failure gives the closing sentence of the Tale an overwhelming bittersweetness because it determines that the child she bears Cupid will be mortal rather than divine.

Voluptas is the highest achievement of unredeemed humanity. As such it is subject to transience and vicissitude: Charite and Tlepolemus die through murder (itself incited by love) and through suicide; the Judgment of Paris is a mythological event whose conclusion was, as Lucius himself reflects, disastrous; the masque itself gives way to the hideous public copulation of murderess and ass.

Even worse, Voluptas is subject to *perversion*, taking the term in a rather more literal sense than usual as connoting a change of normal direction. Something like this fruitful literalism is what we find in *Civilization and*

Its Discontents, where Freud envisions the primal libidnal drive of Eros as a stream and perversion—sadism and masochism—as shifts of course that join Eros with its "immortal adversary." Freud was anticipated in his imagery by an African who broods in his *Confessions* over the perversion of the theater, where men "watch the plays because they hope to be made to feel sad, and the feeling of sorrow is what they enjoy." This shows, Augustine concludes,

> that sorrow and tears can be enjoyable. Of course, everyone wants to be happy; but even if no one likes being sad, is there just the one exception that, because we enjoy pitying others, we welcome their misfortunes, without which we could not pity them? If so, it is because friendly feelings well up in us like the waters of a spring. But what course do these waters follow? Where do they flow? Why do they trickle away to join that stream of boiling pitch, the hideous flood of lust? For by their own choice they lose themselves and become absorbed in it. They are diverted from their true course and deprived of their original heavenly calm.[18]

Apuleius, closer to Freud than to Augustine in his categories, provides us with a similar insight, but all the more vivid for being realized in fiction and for its paratactic "placement" in his narrative. Voluptas is emphatically present in *all* the sexual encounters in the book. In literal translation, Lucius and Fotis spend the night "joining in Voluptas." The servants of the respectable lady who loves an ass move quickly in their preparations so as not to delay "the Voluptas of their mistress." Nor is the recurrence of the term inevitable in a writer whose amorous vocabulary is, if anything, excessively large: as

---

18. Trans. R. S. Pine-Coffin (Harmondsworth, Middlesex: Penguin Books, 1961), p. 56.

a matter of fact, Apuleius tends to reserve the term for the climactic moments of the sexual encounters and tableaus in the *Metamorphoses*. What determines the grotesqueness of these episodes is the admixture of Voluptas with something else: aggression in the case of Fotis (the sustained military language of her encounters with Lucius amounts to more than the "*spectral* sadism" mentioned by Auerbach), self-degradation in the case of the woman enamored of an ass. I shoud add that in scenes not explicitly sexual Apuleius often portrays a root human impulse of destructiveness, unmotivated and self-sustaining, that is very close to Freud's Thanatos.

Voluptas, in the *Metamorphoses,* is a great but limited good. Its symbolic quintessence, the figure of Venus, is fallible in herself and is one goddess among many. Psyche, tormented by a manifestation of Venus in which sadism has virtually swallowed up the positive possibilities of love, turns instinctively in Book 6 to the great goddess who is sister, wife, virgin, and savior. Lucius in Book 11, in the scene anticipated by Psyche's prayer, appeals to the Queen of Heaven, who incorporates all goddesses including Venus. More satisfyingly that Augustine (whose Platonic doctrine of a hierarchy of pleasures is very similar), Apuleius envisions a spiritual life suffused with the tangibility of Voluptas—capable, like Voluptas, of graphic symbolism—and lacking only its genitality, its restlessness, and its cyclical vicissitudes.

The ordering of events in the latter part of Book 10 can now be reassessed. We have already seen how the movement through the four episodes, in its pattern of continual reversal, typifies Apuleius' narrative technique. But it is also a movement out of and into degradation, in which a glimpse of unmodified and undefiled Voluptas is flanked by its own negation. Yet, in a final reversal, one must say that the Venus of the masque is not totally canceled out: she points by implication to the truer Venus of Book 11, the goddess who incorporates Venus as she incorporates all female divinity, and whom Lucius, in an unprecedented triple conversion, incorporates into a yet higher power of unimaginable fullness.

Apuleius' procedure is paratactic and "additive." His message, what we must call his philosophic vision, is all the stronger because there is no statement of message: because it is the reader and not the writer who sparks the gap and makes the work complete.

iii

Thus far we have been circling steadily around the most remarkable portion of the *Metamorphoses,* the Tale of Cupid and Psyche that makes up almost a quarter of its total length. Moving "outward" from the Tale of the Bailiff in Book 8, and now inward from the "extremities" of the book, we arrive again at a story that occupies part of Book 4, all of Book 5, and most of Book 6.

Our purpose has been threefold: to establish in detail the repetitive, musical, even hypnotic quality of Apuleius' prose; to establish simultaneously that the *Metamorphoses* does have the form and shape of a hysteron proteron centered on the Tale of the Bailiff; to show, finally, that this symmetry has an internal rhythm of its own, a falling and rising curve that corresponds to the archetypal rhythm of human experience and human myth.

There has been an obvious risk in this procedure, the possibility of seeming to assert what is obviously untrue, that the book is strictly and mechanically organized. The Tale of Cupid and Psyche, and the narrative complex of The Robbers in which it is embedded, provide the best evidence to the contrary. It would be a truism to observe that the Tale recapitulates in outline the pattern of the work as a whole, and that in a variety of ways—most obviously, the inability to control her restless curiosity— Psyche is analogous to Lucius. The Tale has a fullness and independence of development that is simply incompatible with strict mechanical symmetry, especially when we have already located the center of the hysteron proteron in an "off-center" position, in Book 8 rather than Book 5.

At the same time the Tale takes its place in the beautifully subtle rhythm of the work. Its texture is that of counterpoint or dialectic, with fear and contentment, aspiration and defeat, joy and misery, continually playing off against (and succeeding) each other. Its conclusion, a joyful yet shadowed birth, brilliant blue sky with ominous black cloud, is the paradigm of mortality. In its sense of a tremendous yet rigidly limited aspiration, Voluptas is close to the Homeric vision of heroism; in its attempt to break the wide yet encircling chain, Book 11 of the *Metamorphoses* corresponds to Book 24 of the *Iliad*. In the story of Charite and Tlepolemus, which immediately follows that of Cupid and Psyche, the dialectic of joy and terror shifts conclusively in the direction of death; and immediately thereafter we plunge into the nadir of the book's curve, the pilgrimage of catastrophe, the Tale of the Bailiff, the episode of the Syrian priests.

A comparable musical subtlety is evident in the novel's "rising" curve. The pall of death, so continuously present in the earlier section—death, after all, is the very medium

in which the robbers conduct their work—gradually lifts
from the work. First it becomes a strong localized punctua-
tion; then it disappears altogether, to be recalled only
in the story of the murderess at the end of Book 10.
The persistent altruistic sadism of the earlier episodes,
though echoed in the persecution of Lucius by the baker's
wife, is similarly less conspicuous. The events and tales
at the baker's mill give us consecutive pictures of betrayal
without cruelty but with gross mockery and humiliation
(Tale of the Wife's Tub) and betrayal without open
mockery (Tale of the Jealous Husband). The Tale of
the Fuller's Wife, unpleasant as it is, turns the tables
on the betrayers, and the baker himself then takes a
protracted and successful revenge—a crude common-law
justice—on his scheming wife. All of this ends in disaster,
with the baker's death. The rising curve of the book is
punctuated by catastrophe, just as its declining curve
was punctuated (often satirically) by beauty, heroism,
and joy. The poor gardener who is the first to treat Lucius
as a brother, and who extends an exemplary hospitality
to the lost traveler from a nearby village, is unjustly
condemned to death, while the traveler's exemplary sons
meet a heroic (and avenged) death all the more striking
in the way it echoes episodes from the "heroic" combats
of the robbers. (Like the robber Thrasyleon, one brother
is torn to death by dogs; like the robber Lamachus, the
last of the brothers ends his own life in Catonic suicide.)

Running through all the tales and episodes that follow
the Tale of the Bailiff is an issue that closely parallels
that of Voluptas: a concern with mortal justice and mortal revenge, the struggle of unredeemed humanity to
balance its accounts in an unbalanced universe. The Tale
of the Wicked Stepmother in the first half of Book 10,

with its variant of the Phaedra story, is the only moment in the *Metamorphoses* when such a balance seems possible outside the disastrous ledger of vengeance and suicide. The trial in that Tale is a model of fairness (compare the "justice" of the magistrate at the end of Book 1, the mock trial in Book 3, and the routine association of law with injustice at the end of Book 9), the evil are punished, and the story ends with a striking statement: that its conclusion is "worthy of divine justice" (providentiae divinae condignum). Like the appearance of Venus in the masque of the Judgment of Paris, which gives us a quickly qualified glimpse of an uncorrupted Voluptas, the trial in this Tale, by its loneliness in the *Metamorphoses*, suggests the hopelessness of the very vision it raises. But like the Venus of the masque, the vision of justice is not altogether canceled out: it too points to Book 11 and draws us, like the curve of deepening and diminishing horror, like the modified hysteron proteron of themes, to the consummation at the end of the book.

iv

The "modernity" of Apuleius stems precisely from the free and musical structuring that the oral/rhetorical tradition makes possible, a form of experience that we ourselves are most likely to encounter in cinema. What I have called "structural parataxis" is, after all, a form of montage, and we repeatedly encounter in classical literature—most strikingly of all in Homer—something closely akin to the "camera eye" as it emerges from the editing process. In classical literature as in cinema, montage gives us subtle and multifarious ways of experiencing the polarities of human perception: harmony and disharmony, relation and disjunction, similitude and contrast, cohesion and paradox, wholeness and irony. Best of all, montage can move us from a thing to its opposite by tidal stages, bringing us to an emotional participation in the gradual and eventually overwhelming "swell" of an event, an effect previously achievable only through the amplitude of an epic or of the Victorian novel. In this way, cinema, like its epic and novelistic forerunners, connects the particular scenes and events before our eyes with what all of us experience as a general tidal and cyclical rhythm in ourselves and the world.

Apuleius' medium has a message, and that too has a modern ring to it, for more than anything else the book is about the crisis of daily existence in a society that combines high physical mobility with an intense moral claustrophobia. An imagistic map of Apuleian landscape could appropriately portray an open road lined with prisons. The domestic interiors in which the characters pause amid their peregrinations are usually places of danger and betrayal, ranging from the tavern in the very first tale (it is run by a witch) to the house of Milo to the robber's cave to that factory of torment, the baker's mill. The restless movement of Apuleius' characters, torment moving through torment, already has something Dantesque about it; the antecedents of the *Metamorphoses,* like those of the *Inferno,* can be found in the Virgilian underworld, where motion without end is a punishment that uniquely reflects the character of human life in a modern society.

The exact significance that Apuleius has for us will depend not on how we relate to him but on how we relate to ourselves and our own world. The grace of Isis is freely given and comes from above; in accepting it Lucius is effectively removed from the appalling society he has passed through. A modern reader might be shocked at the ease with which Lucius turns his back on suffering and injustice, or attracted by an Apuleian solution to the pain of his own dilemmas.

3
THE QUEST FOR A BETTER TRADITION: A RETROSPECT

i

To reintegrate Apuleius into our tradition is a good thing, but what does it do to the tradition itself? Can we even begin to conceive of a tradition that gives so central a place to satire and play?

Even in the late 1950s the problem never arose. As an undergraduate at Columbia I was exposed to a "humanities" curriculum which included Homer, Aeschylus, Sophocles, Euripides, Plato, Virgil, Augustine, Boethius, Dante, Shakespeare, and Milton. We read them in chronological order and had a strong if usually implicit sense that each "came out of" his predecessors, the temple of the Western Tradition rising stone on stone to its consummation in the sky.

It was very awesome, also slightly fatiguing; had Columbia undergraduates been less inclined to argue and quibble about everything that came to their attention, it might have been positively dull. As it was I found myself responding more strongly to *Middlemarch* than to the

Iliad. Homer, if truth be told, left a rather blurred impression on my mind, Virgil and Dante I regarded with something bordering on repugnance. It all seemed so *predictable*. Working one's way through the pages one had to admit that people were getting killed or maimed or orphaned, but even death, one sensed, was so much mortar and stone for the tradition. It was death with *a point*, perhaps even a moral, provided for the education of people who knew in their bones that life was pointless; heroic agonies for a generation which already knew that in the modern world people died—whether in bed or behind barbed wire—like roaches, and that the main problem posed by death was now disposal of the corpses.

There were exceptions to the fatigue, of course, but they seemed not to fit into the tradition at all. Shakespeare, for example, was an embarrassment in the otherwise straight thoroughfare from Homer to Milton. One *worked one's way through* Virgil or Milton, noting down the "points" that would have to be made in class ("How does Virgil's vision of the hero differ from Homer's?"), but one fell into a Shakespeare play like a sinner into the hands of an angry god. Not that Shakespeare was angry (one wondered whether he was anything at all), or even universally comprehensible to a mind still mildewed from high school. The point was that he manipulated his reader in a way one couldn't pin down, at once engrossingly and elusively, as if one were blundering about in the middle of a celestial ballet.

Donne was easier to handle—one could read the poem over several times, and annotate it into shape—and here even the orthodoxies of criticism had to take account of an anti-traditional strain in our literature. Donne, we were told in all solemnity, represented a reaction against

Petrarch. The vision of Petrarch that then hatched out in my mind, of a portly little fellow in a long gown permanently frozen into an orator's stance, has prejudiced me against him ever since. But all that was irrelevant. Donne spoke to us directly because he was funny even when he was being serious. Instead of adding his little brick to the fortress of tradition he eroded, or undermined, or exploded the whole affair. The tradition was work and Donne was play. It must have been trying for our instructors to try to "move us on" to *Paradise Lost* and find us grumpy and unwilling.

What was going on at Columbia was an early version of our own grapple (to the death?) between youth and age. Age pointed to the tradition and told us it was important; youth resisted, or quarried the tradition for the very materials with which to repudiate it. The romantic argument that Milton was of the Devil's party looked irresistibly fascinating; the romantics themselves were eternally youthful. Shakespeare was young and Milton was old; Donne was young and Pope was old; Apuleius was young and Augustine was old. They didn't seem part of the "curriculum," but closer to the "extracurricular" world of college humor, practical jokes, derision, and risk—a world that stood in exact counterpoise to the tensions of the "serious" classroom. I say "serious," not "oppressive," because in a part of ourselves we felt guilty about our philistinism, our ignorance, our refusal to respond fully to the banquet laid before us. Often one could even generate a kind of fascination *out of* hostility, a maneuver that today's young would probably find positively perverted. I became adept at writing a kind of analysis which showed why we were unable to respond very enthusiastically to Dryden or Thomson, and putting at least a part of the blame on ourselves. Perhaps this could be called in retrospect the Postlapsarian School of literary criticism. Though I didn't fully realize it at the time, it was a version of what Arnold, Ruskin, Chesterton, Belloc, and T. S. Eliot had been writing for a century.

The strategies that kept us alive and merry while we were led through the tradition never broke the essential hostility between it and us, youth and age. And in a way we were enmeshed in a struggle that mirrored microcosmically the fight between New and Old Critics, a struggle which itself had the connotation of the young battling their elders. At the same time our patchwork resistance coincided with the fundamental split introduced into American society by the Second World War and the Cold War.

By shrugging off the weight of history and biography, with all its fraudulent appeals to nationalism and snobbery (for example, the Wasp adulation of the "English-speaking peoples"), the New Critics freed themselves and their followers to talk about things subversive, ironic, complex, and ambiguous. Frank Kermode is very far from being or having been a New Critic, but his comments on Shakespeare's primal "perversity" would be unimaginable without their work. The New Critics made it possible for us to extend backward an obvious truth about *modern* art and literature, that the artist can exist in an adversary relationship to his society. And by showing us that we should "trust the tale and not the teller," they freed particular novels and poems from the sometimes intolerable stupidities expressed by their creators in letters and lectures.

At the very time that the New Critics were doing this, "humanities" and "great books" courses were being instituted in our colleges. From the start they were defensive in nature, meant to combat the ignorance of the modern freshman, the degrading attractions of mass culture, and the assault mounted against the dignity of man by the Nazis and Communists. They were "elitist" (in the current jargon), and elitism was presented to us as the only way to hold off the threatening forces that had us under siege.

The Cold War, it seemed, had been going on almost since the founding of Athens. Herodotus told how the tradition had been defended in its infancy, Thucydides chronicled a setback, but with Virgil and Dante (happily seconded by Augustus and Aquinas) the tradition got firmly to its feet. Dante, indeed, was the definitive poet of Christendom. Shakespeare kept the tradition alive by exemplifying the Elizabethan World Picture, in which the Great Chain of Being made a place for everyone and kept everyone contentedly in his place. T. S. Eliot, who told us all how sadly we had declined by trying to abandon the verities, hierarchies, and unities of the Middle Ages, was the tradition's last defender against the barbarian, variously represented as the godless commissar, the typist home at teatime, and the Jew. (Rather a shame, that, since most of us were Jewish.)

At Columbia the New Critical and Traditional points of view collided head-on in the curriculum, but the collision was never acknowledged. We *practiced* New Criticism on *parts* of the tradition, mostly those that came under the heading of Eng. Lit., though also on such pleasantly subversive authors as Euripides, Apuleius, Diderot, and Mann. The result was an overriding intellectual incoherence, about which we were too polite to talk. I suppose there is some appropriateness in the fact that we graduated the very year that Northrop Frye's *Anatomy of Criticism* was published. Whatever the faults of that largely unreadable encyclopedia, it at least drove home the point that there was something radically wrong about our ways of talking about literature.

ii

But something was afoot in the 1950s and 1960s that has tended to heal the split in our criticism. Most important of all was the sense of a general national and international crisis with a profound ideological content (though confusingly intermingled with traditional military and geopolitical concerns). The New Critics were always open to attack from academic conservatives as the radical godfathers of a new countercultural ignorance, and from the Left as fraudulently apolitical conservatives who, by denying art its political content, were in fact supporting the status quo. Now there was a new and growing interest in the connections between art, culture, and politics. Precisely to the extent that we felt ourselves floundering as a society, we became more interested in societal "wholes" as they have existed on this planet.

There was an obvious nostalgic element in this, a tendency to recapitulate the socio-aesthetic yearnings of the Gothic Revival. The roots of a writer like Siegfried Giedion, in *Mechanization Takes Command* (1948), are confessedly in the nineteenth century, and his postlapsarian sense of Victorian furnishing and decoration can be compared to the comparable "fall of man" in writers like Ruskin, Arnold, Nietzsche, Spengler, and T. S. Eliot. A kind of critical nostalgia for medieval communalism is the binding thread in Paul Goodman's work. Even a scholarly book like Hans Baron's *The Crisis of the Italian Renaissance* (1966) has at its core an admiration for the communal and "medieval" humanism of Florence, and a concomitant hostility to the imperial tyranny of Milan and its humanist apologists.

Yet the revival of interest in societal "wholes" had some new and notable features. For one thing, it had little of the earlier prejudice against consciousness. The tendency in the nineteenth and early twentieth centuries was to assume that because the writer was trapped in the *angst* and paralyzing self-awareness of modern man, those he was nostalgically writing about—the men of medieval Florence or Periclean Athens—must have been characterized by a "healthier" unconsciousness, a more natural and spontaneous relation of thought and action. (The sexual undertone was always present, especially where the Greeks were concerned.) Now the pendulum swung rapidly in the opposite direction, a tendency paradigmatically represented by Lynn White's *Medieval Technology and Social Change*. White demonstrated that the Middle Ages were technologically progressive, that even the astounding series of refinements and technical solutions responsible for the modern clock were completed before the dawn of the Renaissance. "Medieval man," hitherto envisioned as a peasant contentedly plowing at his appropriate post on the Great Chain of Being, was suddenly a canny technician experimenting at a workbench. At almost the same time, Meyer Schapiro could write of medieval people as conscious aestheticians perfectly capable of "distancing" themselves from their creations (so much for the creative swoon in an Age of Faith). Writers as diverse as E. H. Gombrich, D. W. Robertson, and Paul

Goodman have tended to restore to the medieval artist and thinker an essentially *critical* capacity, and the countervailing critique of the post-medieval world is now that it thinks too little rather than that it reasons too much. One immensely significant result of this tendency has been to alter our balance of thought and action in the direction of the latter. As long as unconscious medieval *praxis* was opposed to the paralyzing rationalism of the modern world, the appropriate role of a modern cultivated man was obviously to admire and appreciate a glorious past when action was still possible. Once criticism and creation ceased to be seen as mutually exclusive faculties, and the stigma of innate inferiority had been removed from "the modern," individual men found that they now had a warrant for action (not necessarily in directions generally approved).

Another significant change in the 1950s and '60s was in our sense of the active role of the artist in his society. The first great wave of nostalgia for a "whole" society gave us the ultimately tautological sense that the artist "reflects" his society and is organically—metapersonally—intertwined with it. Thus, Arnold characteristically insisted that the achievement of a Pericles or a Sophocles sprang from "a national glow of life" in Athens itself. If one asked for proof of that "national glow of life" the answer was obvious: look at Sophocles and Pericles. In Carlyle's vision of the statesman or artist as hero, one can follow a significant cognitive slippage through all the obsessive metaphors of release and control: the titanic heroic energies of a Danton or a Mirabeau spring from a vast social upheaval, a "national glow of life" in the volcanic rather than the solar sense; somehow these energies are transferred to and incarnated in a hero who ultimately controls

and directs them; as a result, repression becomes libera-
tion, since an organic entity cannot be said to repress *itself*. (Thus Carlyle gave Rousseauist notions of the General Will the reactionary tinge they have had ever since.)
The net effect of Carlyle's presentation, despite the wor-
shipful stance toward Dante or Danton, was to deny the
artist and statesman an autonomous role as an actor *upon*
his society, one who incarnates only his *own* will and
seeks, however sympathetically, to influence the wills of
others.

Parallel developments in the nineteenth century can be
found in Tolstoy's vision of history, so close in its essence
to modern geopolitics with its sense of the "eternal" pressure of national and geographical entities on each other,
and in the Darwinian sense of gradual evolutionary
"process." The essential background to all of these patterns was the repudiation of miracle and divine interven-
tion as forces in history, whether the history was cultural,
political, or biological. Gradually, as atheist scholarship
shifted to the offensive, the monomaniacal concern for
gradual evolution and development cast beyond the pale
of respectability anything sudden or unexpected in human
affairs. If the French Revolution was so violent and volcanic an upheaval, then, Carlyle concluded, it must have
been centuries in the making, with the "crust" of the
French ruling class breaking up in a protracted decadence.
If Sophocles or Phidias accomplished something of great
significance, then, Arnold concluded, there must have
been a long and enriching renaissance of thought that
made them possible. The panic-stricken response of the
scientific community to Immanuel Velikovsky, so at odds
with all normal canons of professional ethics, indicates
that this prejudice was still very much alive in 1950, de-

spite the obvious qualifications introduced into our picture of the world by developments like mutation genetics.

Again, the pendulum has swung rapidly—and perhaps too far—in the opposite direction. Marshall McLuhan represents above all an astonishingly crude hunt for first and preferably sudden causes. New Left manichees have converted Marxism from a drama of cosmic "development" to a melodrama of heroes and villains. But these discouraging signs of a new savagery ought not to obscure the reentry into our moral universe of the idea of sudden change, the possibility that after all a fundamental event did take place in the Athens of Solon or the Sinai of Moses. As a result we are able to restore heroic stature to artists and statesmen, and to give that heroism a conscious and critical content.

iii

The repudiation of organic unconsciousness as a fundamental quality of Periclean Athens or the Middle Ages, and our new accessibility to the idea of sudden change in history, are developments that clearly reinforce each other. A third development in recent years has been more difficult to integrate into cultural history, and the difficulty is epitomized in the study of Virgil.

Writing in 1940, in his revisionist study *The Roman Revolution,* Sir Ronald Syme fully accepted the traditional view of Virgil as a participant in the "National Programme" of Augustus. Syme's pioneering study of Roman politics, with its jaundiced concern for political realities and the propaganda that is simultaneously their mask and their revelation, merely shifted the label on Virgil from moral tutor to propagandist, a shift quite in keeping with Syme's astringent sense that all politics is ultimately oligarchical. At almost the same time, C. N. Cochrane, in *Christianity and Classical Culture,* argued that Virgil more than Augustus formulated the central tenets of *Romanitas*—that Augustus' genius lay precisely in recognizing to what use the *Aeneid* could be put.

Since that time the revolution in Virgil criticism seems rapidly to have undermined the very basis of their judgments. The view of the *Aeneid* synoptically produced in recent years by writers like Adam Parry and Michael Putnam leaves us with a deliberately inconclusive poem that never "tells" us whether the currency of Aeneas' humanity is worth the achievements it buys, and which seems as devoted to ironizing as to praising the Roman world-mission. When Aeneas returns from Hades through the gate of false dreams, when the closing murder of his (and Rome's) last enemy verbally echoes the persecution of the Trojans that opens the poem, we seem to have entered a realm closer to black humor than to a "National Programme."

And yet the evidence is clear that the *Aeneid* was the formative document of the Augustan settlement, and that it laid the moral basis for what finally came to be called Romania. The problem which this poses for us is not confined to Virgil. A parallel tendency toward satire can be seen in such "national" works as Shakespeare's *Henry V* and even in the *Iliad* itself; the boundary between "serious" and "frivolous," "tragic" and "satiric," suddenly looks porous and inconclusive.

Clearly it is not enough to say that these works are "like" Apuleius, since they differ from the *Metamorphoses* —overwhelmingly—in their secular purpose, a purpose fully realized in their installation as national curricula.

One way of dealing with the problem is to point, as Northrop Frye does in a recent essay,[19] to the "inclusiveness" of literature that is part of, or close to, the oral tradition, the capacity of such works to include material, perhaps even satirical material, that is unrelated to the primary "point" of the poem. Under this formula, the poet can have his epic and satirize it too, since his audience does not require the tight consistency that we have tended to expect, until recently, of our own literature.

A second and related approach might be to make a strong distinction between the poem "in itself" and the use to which it was subsequently put. "In itself" the poem cannot be constrained within a merely national or propagandistic or moralistic framework, but adroit use of any work can, by emphasizing its positive (that is to say, usable) features and ignoring the others, give it a political direction and utility. The use made of Tolstoy by the Soviets and Nietzsche by the Nazis are cases in point, since they involved relatively little outright bowdlerization; Olivier's film of *Henry V* is another example.

A third and considerably more controversial point of view would be to say that our own sense of national identity as a solemn compact, and of national epics as therefore invested with a uniform moral purpose and an imposing gravity, represents the imposition onto Homer and Virgil of some distinctly nineteenth-century categories, indeed of a particular form of primitivism. Perhaps the crystallizing of national identity in an epic poem can be simultaneously critical/satiric and solemn/tragic. Perhaps, in other words, the moment of crystallization is ex-

---

19. "The Critical Path," *Daedalus* (Spring 1970).

plosively "large," not in the sense that the epic has a baggy inclusiveness, but in the sense of what it can deliberately set out to accomplish.

The suggestion is so controversial because it seems to restore to the epic poet an Olympian stature that we instinctively distrust. Even if we have rejected the cruder forms of historical, biographical, and cultural determinism in literary criticism, we still take for granted the idea that the epic poet, like all artists, is inextricably a part of his time and his culture. If we return to the Renaissance assumption that the earliest poetry is also incomparably the greatest, why not take the final step into absurdity by attributing its greatness to the grace of God, and the fact that the poet carries within him a powerful spark of the divine?

But a crucial issue is glossed over by my formulation "that the epic poet, like all artists, is inextricably a part of his time and his culture." Culture, as we have learned afresh in recent years, is not a stable "given" in human existence. The ideological, intellectual, and national allegiances that enable an individual to locate himself in the universe, are in fact dangerously plastic. Human beings *require* a cultural allegiance in order to exist, but are perfectly capable in times of stress, when one order becomes untenable, of exchanging it for another.

It is probably a truism to say that our greatest artists— Homer, Virgil, Shakespeare, Cervantes, Goethe, Tolstoy— have had as their cultural "moment" precisely such a time of transition. What needs more insistence is that their art characteristically reflects *upon* the process their society is undergoing, and that the process has an extraordinary dialectical character.

Recent events in the United States have brought home

to us the old truth about nationalism, that nationalisms reinforce each other in a mechanism that combines recognition with rejection. There is a moment when X and Y exist side by side, conscious of some basic differences between them, yet not, as they say, "making an issue of it." And there is a moment when the movement of X into a national (defensive/aggressive) self-consciousness stimulates the same process in Y, which in turn reacts back upon, and intensifies, the process in X. The nationalisms that thus emerge are mutually dependent even as their essential point is mutual rejection, the insistence that X cannot be Y and Y cannot be X, and the dependency can even take the form of admiration and introjection, emulation of the very virtues (real or presumed) that make "the other" a formidable competitor. The archetype of the process in modern history is, of course, the European reaction to the Napoleonic conquests. More subtle and suggestive is the relation between American history and American literature: in history, the Negro and the Indian are excluded as fearful dialectical threats, while our literature is studded with homoerotic idylls between white man and red, white man and black.

As the American experience suggests, the dialectic of consciousness ought not to be confined to nationalism in its nineteenth-century (that is to say, territorial) guise, or even to clearly ethnic and linguistic conflicts. What is crucial is the perception of *difference*, and this can be as much cultural as anything else. Indeed, the dialectic can be primarily a collision between value-systems rather than opposed groups; at the same time, opposition between groups tends to sharpen and clarify differences of value.

Thus, the process of human self-definition is laced with irony, even with absurdity. We ourselves have become keenly aware of the fact, since our own identities have moved crucially into flux. Beneath some more obvious sources of anxiety is the central question of where and to what one belongs, and only by answering it can a man determine who he is. But to define one's identity is to exclude the very elements that have provoked one to seek it, so that the alternatives offered to humanity seem to be an anxious and perhaps intolerable "openness" of sensibility or a decisive choice of party, faction, cult, ethnos: a choice that "locks in" the psyche in the very process of granting it peace. Commitment and absurdity are not polar opposites but near cousins on the spectrum of human emotion. Hence the explosive conversion-process in which the modern individual tends to move from anomie and anguished skepticism to the status of true believer, the leap of faith whose paradigm will always be the conversion of Paul.

What we can recognize in a formative national work like the *Iliad*, the *Aeneid*, or *War and Peace*, is an act of imagination that captures this most fundamental of human dilemmas, the anguish of national and personal identity. In each the movement of national affirmation is played off against a contrapuntal wave of regret or sadness or outright irony. Even *War and Peace*, the crest of national feeling in a century of nationalism, incorporates an astonishing and quite Apuleian sense of the unpredictable slipperiness of the world, a sense that is not and cannot be harmonized with orthodox national boosterism: 1812 emerges as a rare harmonious moment in an intrinsically disharmonious world.

One of our most common assumptions is that a questioning and satirical literature represents a second "stage" in cultural development, that Homer is follower by Archilocus, Virgil by Petronius, Milton by Pope, the heroic by the anti-heroic, solemnity by laughter. Concealed within the assumption is an organic analogy: youth is a time for unambiguous commitment, irony and disenchantment is what we acquire with age, and the same ought to be true of the youth and maturity of nations and national literatures. For a variety of reasons the analogy deserves a rest, not the least of them being that it incapacitates us for reading Homer.

4
HOMER

i

What the *Iliad* is about is irremovably subsumed under the question of what the *Iliad* is; and this question seems as mired as ever in the problem of Homer's primitive or sophisticated qualities. Milman Parry's attempt to show that Homer was the product of an oral tradition similar to the one still alive in parts of eastern Europe had a distinctly primitivizing implication. For the oral tradition as he saw it, remarkable as it was in its linguistic breadth and metrical precision, seemed to place the oral poet under immense constraints and to eliminate above all the *originality* that we consider a sine qua non for great poetry. Thus, Parry reintroduced under a new guise the sense of limitation conveyed by the Homeric "Analysts," who saw the epics as anachronistic crazy-quilts, strung together with bits and pieces. A "work" consisting of fragments with visible joints can hardly have an overriding ambition. A "work" dominated by metrical, formulaic, and mnemonic imperatives, themselves the product of nobody-knows-how-many generations of bards, cannot be separated from its very old and authoritarian tradition, and this too makes questions of purpose and point super- fluous.

Yet the conviction has persisted that the Homeric epics somehow extend beyond Parry's categories. The mere fact that the final compilation of the epics must have occurred around the time that alphabetic writing was taken over from the Phoenicians has persistently dis- joined the vision of Homer as a purely and traditionally oral poet. The story that *something* was done to the Homeric text in the time of Solon and Pisistratus has tended to suggest the same thing, that the *Iliad* and the *Odyssey* were perhaps transcribed and revised in the man- ner of a modern novel, and represent the kind of crossing of the oral and written modes that we associate with Shakespeare. Of great though indirect significance have been developments in Biblical scholarship, a growing awareness—epitomized in the Speiser edition and transla- tion of *Genesis*—that disparate materials can be editorially juxtaposed in such a way as to make a unified and co- herent "point." The seams are visible yet they cease to matter.

In recent years, therefore, Homeric scholars have in- creasingly stressed the possibility that Homer, whatever "tradition" he was a product of, did something to it and with it which was of consummate significance.[20] No one has gone further in this line than Cedric Whitman, who sees the *Iliad* as an immense and detailed hysteron proteron. "Not only," he writes, "are certain whole books of the poem arranged in self-reversing, or balancing, de- signs, but the poem as a whole is, in a way, an enormous

20. See as an example, Joseph A. Russo, "Homer Against His Tradi- tion," *Arion* 7 (Summer 1968).

hysteron proteron, in which books balance books and scenes balance scenes by similarity or antithesis, with the most amazing virtuosity."[21] Whitman's diagrammatic presentation of his point, in a fold-out from the back of his book, is bound to evoke a powerful skepticism in anyone who sees it for the first time. What Whitman wants us to believe is that the author of the particular and often transcendentally memorable scenes in the *Iliad* was capable of simultaneously integrating them into a structure of scholastic complexity, a structure that no "oral" audience, however quick-witted, could be expected to appreciate, and whose full development has escaped all previous readers of the *Iliad* in its written or printed form.

It is almost impossible to accept the argument that Whitman offers in *Homer and the Heroic Tradition;* it is also very difficult to refute him. Much of what he says seems documentable in the text itself (though there are some striking weaknesses with which I will deal shortly). But we begin to encounter a profound problem when Whitman presents us with organizational patterns too subtle to be perceived except under the lens of Whitmanian scholarship. The dilemma this poses for him can be traced in the musical analogy that he eventually (like most modern Homeric critics) gets around to making. The analogy is with Mozart, and is at first used to suggest a complete adequacy of communication. Whitman observes that something similar to Homer's achievement

> is perhaps to be found in the style of Mozart. Based as it is on a developed aristocratic tradition, whose compositional elements are largely formulaic, the eighteenth-century manner became in Mozart's hands, through sheer skill of deployment, a medium of surpassing emotional and artistic authority, whose impact is of such intimately combined

21. Whitman, p. 255.

force and elegance that it is hard to say which predominates.[22]

Later the analogy takes a different turn. Struggling to account for the complexity he sees in Homeric structure, Whitman suggests that Homer "seems to have been playing with abstract form for its own sake," and that "we should also ask how many of Mozart's original audiences appreciated the extraordinary economy of tonality in *Don Giovanni,* or caught the musical puns on horns in *Figaro* and *Cosi fan tutte.*"[23]

But there is a world of difference between musical puns, tonal economy, and a system of structure that involves every section, book, and episode of the *Iliad.* Whitman's hypothetical audience could let *Don Giovanni* or *Figaro* wash over them, following the plot and taking pleasure in the music while remaining ignorant of some of its ultimate subtleties. But a literary work, and particularly one organized in the paratactic manner, imposes on its audience a continuous quest for meaning: Why is the author telling me *this?* Why at this point in the work? Where is it going? What shape is emerging and at what point in its development do we find ourselves *right now?* To say that Homer was "playing with abstract form for its own sake," and that his form was not understood until the twentieth century, is to suggest a singular failure of perception in two-and-a-half millennia of readers. Despite their ignorance of its true form, they continued to read it under the quite mistaken impression that it had a coherent shape and form, and that they understood what it was.

Perhaps one ought to reverse chronology and imagine what such a reader might say when confronted with Whitman's chart. Let us imagine more specifically that

22. *Ibid.,* pp. 112–13.
23. *Ibid.,* p. 285.

he focuses on the two books that Whitman himself cites
as the pivotal centers of the *Iliad*, Books 9 and 16.

Each of those books is organized in a pattern of escalating and intensifying action. In Book 9, Achilles is supplicated by the Achaean envoys, Odysseus, Phoenix, and
Ajax, to reenter the battle and save his comrades from
destruction. After the appeal of Odysseus, Achilles seems
actually to intensify his anger, and declares that on the
following morning he will load his ships and leave altogether. After the extraordinary appeal of Phoenix, which
includes a gnomic prophecy of the death of Patroclus, he
postpones a decision on leaving until the next day. After
the much briefer appeal of Ajax, he seems to forget the
possibility of leaving and lays down new and specific conditions for reentering the battle: that he will join his comrades only when Hector and his men reach the Achaean
ships and begin to set them afire.

The escalation is "objective," even formal, in its tripartite development. It is also extraordinarily powerful.
Hanging over the *Iliad* is the triple and connected doom
of Patroclus, of Hector, and ultimately of Achilles himself. The tension in Book 9 is whether this doom, explicitly
foreshadowed in 8.476 and gnomically touched upon in
the supplication of Phoenix, can possibly be averted,
whether Achilles can possibly yield enough to cease col-
laborating in his own doom. He yields, of course, but
conditionally; and the conditions seal that doom once and
for all, just as Oedipus' struggles to avoid the mesh of his
fate only entangle him deeper within it.

Whitman's analysis differs remarkably from this im-
passioned and escalating rhythm of development. His im-
perative is the hysteron proteron, an entirely symmetrical
mode of composition which requires that Book 9 be split
down the middle. So his diagram of the book centers on

the speech of Phoenix, and the bitter irony of Achilles' concession is shifted to a relatively peripheral position, the return of the hysteron proteron to its point of beginning.

Book 16 recapitulates the pattern. Here the Great Battle which has raged since Book 11 reaches its climax in the killing of Patroclus, the Achilles-surrogate, dressed in Achilles' armor, whom Achilles loves with an intensity that transcends all other modes of human relationship. Perhaps only Wagner's *Liebestod* provides an adequate analogy for the way in which this event is approached, prefigured, and introduced in the *Iliad*, the thematic foreshadowing and clarification with which we arrive at it. Yet for Whitman, splitting the book once again down the middle, it centers not on the death of Patroclus but on the elaborate foreshadowing of that death in the killing of Zeus' beloved son Sarpedon.

Whitman's diagrammatic presentation of the *Iliad* as a whole suffers from a similar affliction. His own statement of duocentricity, of an *Iliad* with 24 books that pivots on the 9th and 16th, implies pretty clearly that the work is organized by thirds. But a work organized by thirds has no proper "center" at all. And indeed, the center that Whitman posits for it has a curiously vague quality. On his diagram, it is located at Books "11–15."

There is much that is right in Whitman's brilliant book, and there is something fundamentally wrong, an insight too literally and fanatically applied. We must start over, and we must start elsewhere.

ii

The strangest section of the *Iliad* is Book 10, usually

called the "Doloneia." It is located between the Embassy
to Achilles (with the supplications of Odysseus, Phoenix,
and Ajax) and the onset of the Great Battle, and differs
markedly in style from the remainder of the *Iliad;* it has
often been assumed to be a late interpolation, perhaps as
late as the time of Peisistratus. It consists of roughly three
major episodes: a gathering of the Achaean leaders, with
a strangely mannered and formal description of the armor
donned by each; the night-expedition of Diomedes and
Odysseus against the Trojan camp, and the killing of the
pathetic Trojan warrior Dolon; their attack on the sleep-
ing Thracians, their capture of the magnificent horses
belonging to the Thracian king Rhesus, and their triumphant return to the camp of the Achaeans. The Doloneia seems to derive from nothing and to lead to nothing;
it is unusually brief (579 lines to 713 for Book 9 and 848
for Book 11); it reads like a pastiche or imitation of
Homeric style. The Leaf-Bayfield edition of the *Iliad* puts
the matter with brutal succinctness when it observes that
if the Doloneia had been utterly lost "we should have
had no possible ground for supposing that it had ever
existed."

Yet a careful reader of Book 10 will find his memory
of the *Iliad* continually triggered by what it describes.
The obsession with the arming of the Achaean heroes, for
example, an obsession that even extends to the precise
and curious outfit worn by the hapless Dolon, reminds
one of the detailed arming of Achilles toward the end of
Book 19. In Book 10, Dolon undertakes his expedition to
the Achaean camp because Hector has promised him the
horses of Achilles, and the end of the Doloneia picks up
the theme of horses by showing us the capture of the
superb specimens belonging to Rhesus. Similarly, the very

end of Book 19, immediately subsequent to the arming of
Achilles, focuses on his magnificent horses, one of whom
—Xanthos—prophesies his death. Three lines after the
end of Book 10 we have the appearance of the goddess
Hate, who starts the Great Battle with her terrible cry.
She screams again at the beginning of Book 20, in concert
(this time) with Athene and Ares.

But the strangest aspect of Book 10 is Dolon himself.
I have called him "pathetic" and "hapless," and even these
adjectives suggest the problematic position he occupies
in the *Iliad*. In some ways he resembles the utterly contemptible Thersites: he is unattractive (though not
grotesque), a coward (yet not a commoner). The carica-
ture of Thersites, beaten into a tearful silence by Odysseus, tells us clearly what we ought to think of him. Dolon
elicits a measure of our sympathy. When he flees from
Diomedes and Odysseus, then

as when two rip-fanged hounds have sighted a wild beast,
a young deer, or a hare, and go after it, eagerly always
through the spaces of the woods, and the chase runs
     crying before them,
so the son of Tydeus, and Odysseus, sacker of cities,
kept always hard on his heels and cut him off from his
     people. (10.360–64)[24]

One is reminded of the "fleeings" that dominate Books 20,
21, and 22 of the poem: of Aeneas from Achilles (in recol-
lection), of Achilles from the river Xanthos, of Agenor
from Achilles, of Hektor in the dreamlike chase around

24. All quotations, unless otherwise noted, are from the Lattimore
translation. All quotations from the Greek text have been taken from
the Leaf and Bayfield edition (London: Macmillan and Co., 1895 and
1898).

the walls of Troy. When Dolon, so curiously vulnerable in his armor of animal-hides, supplicates Diomedes and Odysseus for mercy and is killed by the former with a swordstroke to the neck, we are reminded of other supplicating Trojans who are denied mercy in the Great Battle but most of all of the naked Lykaon whom Achilles kills at the beginning of Book 21. And the twelve Thracians killed by Diomedes and Odysseus remind one of the twelve Trojans captured by Achilles in the river Xanthos and immolated on the pyre of Patroclus. He captures them just before he encounters Lykaon.

Book 10 seems clearly tied to the narrative complex that begins with Achilles' reentry into the battle and ends with the death of Hector, a complex that begins at the end of Book 19 and extends through Book 22. If it is in fact a late addition to the poem, then it was inserted by someone who was simultaneously giving the *Iliad* a shape, perhaps the very shape it has today. The arch that extends from the beginning of Book 10 to the end of Book 22 implies that the events between its antipodes are also symmetrically related, and that the events just "outside" it—in Books 9 and 23-24—are similarly connected. A careful reading of the poem establishes precisely this kind of symmetry. Best of all, it need not be attributed to Homer's use of "abstract form for its own sake." Its shape and its symmetry are intimately related to the meaning of the poem, to what Homer is trying to tell us, a message that has lost none of its relevance or power.

iii

What the *Iliad* is about is human relation and disrelation. The paradigm of disrelation is the warfare between

Achaean and Trojan, an escalating agon of hatred that finally legitimizes every atrocity committed against the dehumanized and dialectically excluded Other. The paradigm of relation is that between parent and child.

In the order of war the inevitable admired qualities are those of what we now call a "shame culture." To be strong, not to lose face before one's peers, to make oneself *exterior* like a fortress wall, to be unwavering and immovable—to be all these things is to be an ideal man. To be Thersites is to be none of them.

But the order of parent-and-child brings with it a terrible vulnerability. The parent who fears for his child, like Priam pleading with Hector to escape Achilles, stands at the polar extreme from heroism. The child in relation to his parents, even if the child is Achilles and full-grown, is similarly plunged into a mire of helplessness. It remembers its own time of vulnerability; it is confronted with the terrible paradox of old age, the restoration of childish helplessness to a human being who has experienced his heroic prime.

The *Iliad,* so much of which is about the order of war, begins and closes with the order of parent-and-child. In Book 1, at the very threshold of all that is to come, the priest Chryses supplicates the Achaeans for the ransom of his daughter and is brutally refused by Agamemnon. He is an old man. In Book 24 the old king Priam comes as a suppliant to Achilles to recover the body of his son:

"Honor then the gods, Achilleus, and take pity upon me
remembering your father, yet I am still more pitiful;
I have gone through what no other mortal on earth has
gone through;
I put my lips to the hands of the man who has killed my
children."

So he spoke, and stirred in the other a passion of
    grieving
for his own father. He took the old man's hand and
    pushed him
gently away, and the two remembered, as Priam sat
    huddled
at the feet of Achilleus and wept close for manslaughtering
    Hektor
and Achilleus wept now for his own father, now again
for Patroklos. The sound of their mourning moved in the
    house. (24.503–12)

In the web of mourning, and with a Kierkegaardian
abruptness, the barrier between Trojan and Achaean
comes down. Disrelation gives way to relation. Priam
assumes a strange symbolic fatherhood over his son's
murderer, and Achilles becomes Priam's son.

From the beginning of Book 9 to the end of Book 24
we are seldom allowed to forget the theme of parent-and-
child and the associated theme of blood kinship. The
Great Battle differs from the high-spirited heroics in
Books 2 through 8 precisely because it brings the order
of war and the order of parent-and-child into an unbear-
able conjunction. When Ajax kills Hippothous over the
body of Patroclus—a "minor killing"—we are told nothing
about him but the hideous manner of his death and that
"he could not/render again the care of his dear parents;
he was short-lived,/beaten down beneath the spear of
high-hearted Aias." (17.301–3) At the beginning of Book
18, Thetis hears her son Achilles plot the death of Hector
in vengeance for Patroclus; she anticipates her mourning
over him at the very moment that he is mourning
Patroclus. Lattimore's translation mimics precisely the
plangency and simplicity of the Greek:

Then in turn Thetis spoke to him, letting the tears fall:
"Then I must lose you soon, my child, by what you are
    saying,
since it is decreed your death must come soon after
    Hector's." (18.94–96.)

When Achilles kills Lykaon and flings his body into the
river Scamander (Xanthus), the summit of his gloating
over the body is that Lykaon's mother will not be able
to lay him on his death-bed and mourn over him. The
dying Hector supplicates Achilles "by your knees, by your
parents,/do not let the dogs feed on me by the ships of
the Achaians" and receives a reply that echoes Achilles'
gloating over Lykaon:

"not if Priam son of Dardanos should offer to weigh out
your bulk in gold; not even so shall the lady your mother
who herself bore you lay you on the death-bed and mourn
    you:
no, but the dogs and the birds will have you all for their
    feasting." (22.351–54)

And as the body of Patroclus is consumed on its pyre,
we are told that Achilles' mourning is like that of a father
who "mourns as he burns the bones of a son, who was
married/only now, and died to grieve his unhappy parents. . . ."

As in Apuleius, the texture of Homer's narrative consists of densely interwoven echoes and analogies. No
event or encounter loses its integrity, yet each is connected with others, and all are connected with the central
moments of the *Iliad*, the unforgettable scenes that climax
and conclude in Book 24. And as in Apuleius, the final
leap of the book, so persistently anticipated and pre-

figured in what has gone before, carries us to a new level of being altogether. In the very act of mourning their blood kin, Priam and Achilles move beyond the limits of blood kinship and are joined to each other in an emblem of transfigured humanity. Blood kinship carries with it the inevitable corollary of blood vengeance. Under its iron rule, Priam and Achilles owe each other only death. What happens before our eyes is that the antipodes of hostility abruptly give way to the unlimited ecumenism of man. The iron wall between men becomes a porous membrane, and the *Iliad* the record of a conversion.

But in the great arch that extends from Book 9 to Book 24, and has as its keystone the death of Patroclus, even this final leap of sensibility is prefigured and foreshadowed. To see the astonishing way in which this is done we must begin with Book 9.

iv

It is Agamemnon and not Achilles who initiates the tragedy of the Achaeans, driving the old priest Chryses away with threats and bringing the vengeance of Apollo down on his comrades. *Menin aeide, thea, Peleiadeo Achilleos,* reads the first line of the *Iliad*: "The wrath sing, O goddess, of Achilles son of Peleus" (my translation). But the *menis* of Achilles is triggered by a process of escalation as relentless as that of the *Iliad* itself. Kalchas the prophet, when Achilles asks him in the assembly to explain the behavior of Apollo, refers to the *menin Apollonos,* and when he has put the blame on Agamemnon, and the latter rises to speak, the word fairly crackles through the description of his appearance and moves into assonance with his very name:

>   toisi d' anestei
> heros Atreides euru kreion Aga*memnon*
> achnu*menos. Meneos* de mega phrenes amphi melainai
> pimplant'. . . .

>   and among them stood up
> Atreus' son the hero wide-ruling Agamemnon
> raging, the heart within filled black to the brim with anger
> from beneath. . . . (1.101–4)

Agamemnon's bitter speech embraces his fate. He wants the daughter of Chryses in his own house, as servant and bedmate, because "I like her better than Klytaimestra/my own wife." To the audience of the *Iliad* it is instantly comprehensible that a man who speaks in this way, and who begins his address with the sputtering hatred of *Manti kakon, ou po pote moi to kreguon eipas,* "Seer of evil: never yet have you told me a good thing," will return from Troy to be murdered by the wife he scorns. Of more immediate significance is the *menis* that he induces in Achilles, a wrath that stops barely short of murder.

So reprehensible is Agamemnon in Book 1 that his behavior here has often dominated his character sketch in the writings of Homeric scholars. To do this is to impose *stasis* on a work that is the epitome of motion. In its tragic espect the *Iliad* is the tragedy not of Agamemnon but of Achilles, and from the end of Book 1 the portrait of Agamemnon etched on our minds by the conflict with Achilles is softened and blurred. There is nothing arbitrary about the process. Agamemnon, we

come to understand, is not a villain but a man whose
anger derives from insecurity, a blunderer who can be
pathetically anxious to make amends. In Book 4, when
his typically fussy interference in the preparations for
battle angers Odysseus—a far less dangerous opponent,
let it be noted, than Achilles—then

Powerful Agamemnon in turn answered him, laughing,
seeing that he was angered and taking back the word
　　　spoken:
"Son of Laertes and seed of Zeus, resourceful Odysseus:
I must not be niggling with you, nor yet give you orders,
since I know how the spirit in your secret heart knows
ideas of kindness only; for what you think is what I think.
Come now, I shall make it good hereafter, if anything evil
has been said; let the gods make all this come to nothing."
　　(4.356–63)

There could not be a stronger contrast to the Agamemnon of Book 1, or a speech more obviously intended to
call our attention to the change in the speaker. We know
it, but Achilles does not. In this way the stage is set
for the most complex of Homer's achievements in the
Iliad, the achievement of Book 9.

No book in the poem shows more striking signs of having been reworked in the final compilation of the *Iliad.*
The entire book may have been a late insertion into the
poem, and the figure of Phoenix, whose supplication of
Achilles dominates its central section, is clearly an even
later insertion into the book. The "seams" are almost
grossly obvious: only portions of the Old Testament give
such clear evidence of reediting in an important text.
The first mention that Phoenix receives in the *Iliad* is
when Nestor appoints him as the head of an embassy
whose subordinate members are Ajax and Odysseus! Yet

the envoys are persistently referred to thereafter as being two in number, and Phoenix is only perfunctorily mentioned until the moment he begins his extraordinary supplication. After Odysseus, Phoenix, and Ajax have pleaded with him, Achilles' final (and fatal) conditions are that he will not fight until the Trojans reach the Achaean ships and set them ablaze. But the report of the embassy that Odysseus gives to Agamemnon mentions only the speech that Achilles made after the initial supplication by Odysseus himself; it shows no awareness at all of the successive "movements" of Achilles, the formal pattern of concession that the reader has just encountered.

The result is to set in bolder relief the point and purpose of the *Iliad*. Book 9 begins with an Agamemnon "stricken at heart with the great sorrow," a man so contrite that he meekly accepts the public rebukes of Diomedes and Nestor. In conference with the Achaean lords, he offers amends that verge on the hyperbolical. We seem to have reached the apogee of the counter-movement that began at the end of Book 1, the gradual shift in the balance of justification from Achilles to Agamemnon. But a completed shift of this kind would free Achilles from the web of necessity: mere pigheadedness is no basis for tragedy. And so Agamemnon ends his speech of contrition with four lines that read like an eruption—stuttering, choppy, resentful—and that abruptly reveal to us the old Agamemnon:

dmetheto—Aides toi ameilichos ed' adamastos.
touneka kai te brotoisi theon echthistos apanton—
kai moi huposteto, hosson basileuteros eimi
ed' hosson genei progenesteros euchomai einai.

Let him give way. For Hades gives not way, and is pitiless,

and therefore he among all the gods is most hateful to
 mortals.
And let him yield place to me, inasmuch as I am the
 kinglier
and inasmuch as I can call myself born the elder. (9.158–
 61)

Lattimore quite fails to capture Agamemnon's voice. In
the first half of the third line the emphasis of the English
falls on "place," while the Greek falls on what is truly
crucial: *moi,* "me," the self that has had to be beaten
down because the Achaeans are being beaten on the
battlefield.

When Odysseus reports Agamemnon's offer to Achilles
he prudently omits this concluding demand, but Achilles
seems to intuit its having been made; and his extraordinary harangue, in which he compares his fighting and
looting for the Achaeans to the efforts of a mother bird
bringing food to her chicks, climaxes with the statement
that he will sail for home on the following morning. He
answers the eruption of Agamemnon with an explosive
vehemence of his own. Even the details of his language
begin to recall the stinging insults he hurled at Agamemnon in Book 1.

But Achilles' speech also reveals a growth in complexity and self-knowledge, a kind of inner division that
has carried him far beyond the monolithic heroism of
his earlier condition. In Book 1 Achilles is a dealer of
death, and the decision posed to him is whether or not
to kill the man who insulted him; taking for granted
the fact of his short life, he complains only of being
deprived of a commensurate glory. Achilles' speech in
reply to Odysseus is laced with images of death, but its
concern is with receipt rather than delivery. The fact of

his own death has become concrete to him, and he has established a kind of dialogue with it, even a kind of dialectic in which the awareness of death embellishes, intensifies, and complexifies the self and makes death all the more terrible a paradox. "A man's life cannot come back again," he cries out in anguish to Odysseus, stating the most terrible of truisms, "it cannot be lifted/ nor captured again by force, once it has crossed the teeth's barrier." Achilles has discovered the human condition, at least to the extent that he is able to apply it to himself. His desire to sail home the following day is the desire not to die, to choose long life over short and a humdrum existence over glory.

Yet there are aspects of death that have not yet occurred to him. Enclosed in the wall of his new self he thinks of death as a personal loss. Only the death of Patroclus will show him what death means in the context of relationship, and how it condemns the survivor to death-in-life. Even then he will only have reached the halfway point in his pilgrimage. In Book 24 he will learn that what is true of Achilles deprived of Patroclus is true of those he has deprived by his killings: that in the fullest context of death there are no sides or factions, only the harmony of loss.

5
THE SUPPLICATION OF PHOENIX

i

Phaidim' Achilleu, Phoenix calls him in the opening of his supplication, "glorious Achilles," and *philon tekos,* "dear child." The formulaic epithet, Achilles' public self, plays off against a level of private awareness that sees in Achilles still the vulnerable being he has seemingly outgrown.

In the Greek of Homer a man carries his father with him in his name in a manner that can subordinate and even submerge his own identity. *Peleiadeo Achilleos* in the opening line of the poem, usually translated as "Achilles son of Peleus," carries in the original a more compressed possessive force: "Achilles of Peleus," or "Peleus' Achilles." When Patroclus makes his first appearance in the poem he has no name of his own at all: he is *Menoitiades,* "of Menoitios," all son and no self.

It is all the more striking, therefore, that Phoenix is Achilles' adoptive rather than blood father, the man whom Peleus assigned to raise him, and that his tormented history is that of a man severed from his own father by an unspeakable Oedipal conflict and barred forever from having children of his own. He reminds his "dear child" how he had to flee from Hellas

running from the hatred of Ormenos' son Amyntor,
my father; who hated me for the sake of a fair-haired
    mistress.
For he made love to her himself, and dishonoured his
    own wife,
my mother; who was forever taking my knees and entreat-
    ing me
to lie with this mistress instead so that she would hate the
    old man.
I was persuaded and did it; and my father when he heard
    of it straightway
called down his curses, and invoked against me the
    dreaded furies
that I might never have any son born of my seed to dandle
on my knees; and the divinities, Zeus of the underworld
and Persephone the honoured goddess, accomplished his
    curses. (9.448–57)

The result was a murderous anger that brought him to the verge of parricide, the first moment in his speech when we sense an analogy to the *Iliad* as a whole. Phoenix's anger against his father was checked by "some one among the immortals," as Achilles in Book 1 was checked by Athene in the very act of drawing his sword. Phoenix's kinsmen kept him locked within his house (one is reminded of Achilles' self-imposed imprisonment within his tent) lest his rage break out again, and supplicated him endlessly (as Achilles is being supplicated by his comrades), and kept watch over him successfully for nine

days (as nine years have elapsed before Troy). On the
tenth night he escaped.

Then I fled far away through the wide spaces of Hellas
and came as far as generous Phthia, mother of sheepflocks,
and to lord Peleus, who accepted me with good will
and gave me his love, even as a father loves his own son
who is a single child brought up among many possessions.
He made me a rich man, and granted me many people,
and I lived, lord over the Dolopes, in remotest Phthia,
and, godlike Achilleus, I made you all that you are now,
and loved you out of my heart, for you would not go
    with another
out to any feast, nor taste any food in your own halls
until I had set you on my knees, and cut little pieces
from the meat, and given you all you wished, and held the
    wine for you.
And many times you soaked the shirt that was on my body
with wine you would spit up in the troublesomeness of
    your childhood.
So I have suffered much through you, and have had much
    trouble,
thinking always how the gods would not bring to birth
    any children
of my own; so that it was you, godlike Achilleus, I made
my own child, so that some day you might keep hard
    affliction from me. (9.478–95)

Adopted by Peleus, Phoenix adopts Achilles. But surrogate fatherhood is somehow more intense than that of
blood, hermaphroditic in its intensity as Phoenix performs
not only a father's but a mother's functions. One is reminded of what the ghost of Patroclus will recall to
Achilles in Book 23. Patroclus too had to flee his home,
having killed a playmate accidentally as a child. He too
was adopted by Peleus. He too was no blood kin to the

man who loved him so passionately in life and cannot sufficiently avenge him in death. Symbolic kinship can be stronger than blood. Achilles' relationships with Phoenix and Patroclus prepare us for the bonds that he forges with Priam in Book 24 and the ultimate ecumenism of the *Iliad*, the closing chord of dialectical strife.

Phoenix's recapitulation of his history forms the first section of his appeal. The second is devoted to an equally surprising theme, unheard of in the earlier books of the poem, which is the idea that a man must yield when he is supplicated, must compromise even his heroic selfhood rather than try to exact the full price of his anger. In effect Phoenix demands the replacement of a heroic by a social principle: not the explosive "shame culture" that we see in Book 1, whose demands of pride and face assure continual disruption, but a community of selfrepressed and subautonomous individuals. Phoenix even maintains that this is the way things were "in the old days also, the deeds that we hear of/from the great men, when the swelling anger descended upon them./The heroes would take gifts; they would listen, and be persuaded."

Phoenix's assertion, perhaps the most unprovable in the poem, is the bridge to the third and longest section of his supplication, the story of Meleager. Only in Apuleius can one find a comparable density of echo and analogy: it is a parable that reaches out in every direction and ultimately brings the entire *Iliad* into its embrace.

The circumstances of the story parallel point for point the events of the *Iliad*. Oineus, king of the Aetolians whose capital is Calydon, angered the goddess Artemis by failing to give her the first fruits of his orchards. Artemis sent a fierce wild boar to ravage the land, as Apollo ravages the Achaeans with his arrows (perhaps

to point up the allusion, Artemis is explicitly called the
"Lady of Arrows"). Meleager succeeded in killing the
boar, but Artemis made a quarrel break out between
Kouretes and Aetolians over the boar's head and hide, and
the result was a war that both parallels and inverts the
situation at Troy. In obvious significant ways Meleager
"is Achilles": he is supreme in battle and holds off the
Kouretes until anger causes him to withdraw from the
battle; he receives a triple supplication to return, from
the elders and priests of Aetolia, from his parents and
sisters, and finally from his own friends. He refuses them
all. Then, when the Kouretes are actually climbing the
walls and firing the city, he succumbs to the supplication
of his wife Cleopatra, but it is too late: though he succeeds in driving off the Kouretes, he gets no presents
at all.

As an almost literal recapitulation of the larger action
in the poem, the parable of Meleager is both startling
and disappointing. What is disappointing is the flatness
of the conclusion. The opening portion of Phoenix's supplication, in which he conjures Achilles by the deepest
bonds of which humanity is capable, seems to tail off
into a concern with gifts that returns us to the level of
appeal in Odysseus' speech. What is startling is the
audacity with which the parable puns on the name of
Patroclus, and establishes the relationship between
Meleager and his wife as analogical to that between
Achilles and his friend. Cleopatra is Patroclus (the Greek
forms are Patroklos/Kleopatra); the parable reminds us
in passing, and in a rather confusing manner, that her
name was originally Alcyone and gives no reason for the
change, there being no reason other than the necessities
of the pun that Homer is creating.

The great arch that extends from Book 9 to Book 24 has as its keystone the killing of Patroclus, and the action of his death begins when he supplicates Achilles to return to the battle, or, failing that, to permit him to wear his armor and impersonate Achilles in the combat. What motivates Patroclus at that point is pity for the sufferings of the Achaeans, a pity so intense that he "wept warm tears, like a spring dark-running/that down the face of a rock impassable drips its dim water."

In precisely the same way, Cleopatra supplicated Meleager "in tears, and rehearsed in their numbers before him/all the sorrows that come to men when their city is taken." But the parallel is even closer and extends to the inversion of sex. The subject of Greek pederasty having endlessly agitated mankind, it is hard to be certain of the precise sexual implication behind the Patroclus/Cleopatra pun. What is quite certain and documentable is the response of Achilles in Book 16 when Patroclus appears before him in tears:

"Why then
are you crying like some poor little girl, Patroklos,
who runs after her mother and begs to be picked up
    and carried,
and clings to her dress, and holds her back when she
    tries to hurry,
and gazes tearfully into her face, until she is picked up?
You are like such a one, Patroklos, dropping these soft
    tears.
Could you have some news to tell, for me or the Myr-
    midons?
Have you, and nobody else, received some message from
    Phthia?
Yet they tell me Aktor's son Menoitios lives still

and Aiakos' son Peleus lives still among the Myrmidons.
If either of these died we should take it hard." (1.6–16)

Achilles' speech on the very threshold of the doom of
Patroclus makes one suddenly sharply aware that the
dialectic of the *Iliad* includes a sharp separation between
male and female roles. Patroclus in his pity (we have
seen it before in book 11, when he abandons his mission
to treat the wounded Eurypylus, and in Book 15, when
he is rediscovered at the latter's bedside), though it
clearly has no effect on his capacities as a warrior, is
instinctively seen by Achilles as a womanish quality.
Achilles' judgment seems the normative one of his society, the "shame culture" of Book 1 that stereotypes
its heroes along narrow channels of pride and face. Like
Phoenix, Patroclus transcends the limits of his society by
transcending the established limits of his sexual role.
Phoenix is mother and father in his relation to Achilles,
and Patroclus is warrior and woman in his relation to
his fellow Achaeans. Fatherless and bisexual, they have
broken the fundamental separating walls imposed by
their society, walls that are analogical in their operation
to the one that separates Achaeans and Trojans. Though
Patroclus never attains the level of sensibility that we see
in Book 24, he has, in Book 16, left Achilles far behind,
as the response of the latter shows when he says, in effect,
that the only cause for weeping is the death of one's
blood father.

The parable of Meleager anticipates all of this and yet,
in the end, seems to trivialize itself away. The transcendence of Patroclus in Book 16 comes moments before
his doom, just as Hector will attain his full stature only
in the moment before his death, just as Book 24 has

hanging over it the unwritten Book 25 of the death of Achilles and Book 26, the fall of Troy. But the supplications of Cleopatra issues only in the fact that Meleager "gave way in his own heart, and drove back the day of evil/from the Aitolians; yet these no longer would make good/their many and gracious gifts; yet he drove back the evil from them."

I have called the parable "disappointing." But we should consider for a moment what the effect would be if it told of the death of Cleopatra, and somehow attributed that death to the actions and inactions of Meleager. Would the *Iliad* still be, by any stretch of the imagination, tragic? To ignore straightforward prophecy is to be not tragic but a fool.

In fact, the doom of Patroclus is touched on in the parable, but in a manner of brilliant and haunting displacement. When the Kouretes are storming Calydon, and Meleager merely lies in bed with Cleopatra, we are given her history, and the history of Meleager's anger, in a passage that touches on a great deal and explains almost nothing:

But when the anger came upon Meleagros, such anger
as wells in the hearts of others also, though their minds
    are careful,
he, in the wrath of his heart against his own mother,
    Althaia,
lay apart with his wedded bride, Kleopatra the lovely,
daughter of sweet-stepping Marpessa, child of Euenos,
and [of] Idas, who was the strongest of all men upon
    earth
in his time; for he even took up the bow to face the King's
    onset,
Phoibos Apollo, for the sake of the sweet-stepping maiden;

a girl her father and honoured mother had named in their
    palace
Alkyone, sea-bird, as a by-name, since for her sake
her mother with the sorrow-laden cry of a sea-bird
wept because Phoibos Apollo had taken her;
with this Kleopatra he lay mulling his heart-sore anger,
raging by reason of his mother's curses, which she called
    down
from the gods upon him, in deep grief for the death of
    her brother,
and many times beating with her hands on the earth
    abundant
she called on Hades and on honoured Persephone, lying
at length along the ground, and the tears were wet on
    her bosom,
to give death to her son; and Erinys, the mist-walking,
she of the heart without pity, heard her out of the dark
    places. (9.553–72)

Here the "history" ends, to be followed with no break or
explanation by the successive supplications of Meleager
to return to the battle. Nothing in this cloudy narrative
is ever clarified, and the Leaf-Bayfield edition has no
hesitation in applying to it the adjectives "superfluous"
and "confused."

Yet from the confusion emerge the twin themes of
mourning and doom. Marpessa wailing over the daughter
whom Apollo has made away with reminds us that when
Patroclus meets his doom it is Apollo who strikes him
from behind and stuns him for the slaughter, and that
when Achilles learns his companion has been killed "he
cried out/terribly, aloud, and the lady his mother heard
him/as she sat in the depths of the sea." Althaia beating
the ground and summoning the vengeance of the chthonic
powers instantly recalls the father of Phoenix who "called
down his curses, and invoked against me the dreaded

furies/that I might never have any son born of my seed to dandle/on my knees; and the divinities, Zeus of the underworld/and Persephone the honoured goddess, accomplished his curses." In these passages Homer turns from the Olympians to the dark gods of the underworld. They cast over the supplication of Phoenix a baleful sense of automatism and vengeance, and in the parable of Meleager suggest a doom that extends beyond the parable itself and that Meleager cannot avert. As images in a solution, the stages of the parable attain a level of gnomic prophecy more applicable to Achilles and Patroclus than the mere events at Calydon suggest.

A final brilliant level in the parable of Meleager remains to be mentioned. In the precise details of his behavior Meleager resembles Achilles, but as the defender of a city he resembles Hector, and as a man willing to lie abed with his wife while others are battling for survival he resembles the Paris whom even Helen comes to scorn. In the final perspective of the *Iliad*, Achilles and Hector, Trojan and Achaean, will at last become interchangeable in their common humanity: the sacker of cities and those whose city is doomed. That perspective is glanced at in the parable, particularly when Cleopatra supplicates Meleager in tears with the "Trojan" vision of "all the sorrows that come to men when their city is taken:/they kill the men, and the fire leaves the city in ashes,/and strangers lead the children away and the deep-girdled women." The words are a Homeric formula but always recall the great scene between Hector and Andromache in Book 6, in which Hector foresees the fate of Troy. Cleopatra's pity for the Aetolians is analogous to the pity of Patroclus for the sufferings of his fellow Achaeans; at the same time she becomes a kind of inverted Andromache offering Hector's vision to a Paris-like hus-

band who is also Achilles. Of all the implications in this
most subtle of parables, this one is, for Achilles, the least
flattering.

ii

The supplication of Phoenix reveals with particular
clarity the directing intelligence of the *Iliad*. It embraces
the poem and encompasses the fate of Achilles; yet, in
its deliberately trivialized conclusion, it leaves Achilles
a free agent. It is the intelligence we encounter again
in the *Oedipus* of Sophocles, when Teiresias refuses to
tell what he knows and Oedipus' character collaborates
seamlessly with his doom.

The framework of Phoenix's supplication, the overt
structuring of its rhetoric, is trivial; its center touches
an infinitely deeper nerve. Achilles' reply is precisely
commensurate with what has provoked it. It is thirteen
lines long, responds only in a superficial manner to what
Phoenix has said, and yet there is within an audible
slippage of gears which suggests a deep unease. Phoenix
has concluded by saying that Achilles, unlike Meleager,
should go to battle with the gifts he has been promised,
since "if without gifts you go into the fighting where
men perish,/your honour will no longer be as great,
though you drive back the battle." Achilles begins his
reply by saying

"Phoinix my father, aged, illustrious, such honour is a
     thing
I need not. I think I am honoured already in Zeus' or-
     dinance
which will hold me here beside my curved ships as long
     as life's wind

stays in my breast, as long as my knees have their spring
   beneath me." (9.607–10)

With startling suddenness the inner conviction keeping
Achilles on his course has vanished. His reply to Odysseus,
a furious denunciation of Agamemnon and his gifts, was
triggered by a passion recapitulating and even exceeding
that of Book 1. In that passion, as in all passion, Achilles
was one with himself, language and feeling inextricably
fused. Here the language suggests a distinct split between
desire and decision. Achilles shifts the burden of decision
from his own shoulders to those of Zeus, suggesting that
it is a force outside himself that keeps him inactive; and
then, in a revealing paradox, swears to remain inactive
as long as his most active faculties—those that make him
"swift-footed Achilles" and invincible in battle—are with
him. What follows now has a force and subtlety barely
glimpsed in Lattimore's translation. First a line of formula, which here suggests the mind marking time and
groping beneath its automatic fluency for an argument
to stand on:

allo de toi ereo, su d' eni phresi balleo seisin

"And put away in your thoughts this other thing I tell
   you" (9.611)

and then a line and a half, with a marked pause at the
end of the first, which I have translated myself:

me moi sungchei thumon oduromenos kai acheuon,
Atreidei heroi pheron charin

"don't confuse my heart with lamentation and grief—
trying to pleasure great Atreides" (9.612–13)

Between what Achilles has "picked up" from Phoenix's

supplication and what he is able to articulate there is
a terrible gap. The intuition knows that something dreadful and threatening has been conveyed, something that
involves lamentation and grief, while the mind can only
rummage through the stale warehouse of its grievances.
Here and elsewhere in the poem—most notably in his
dialogue with Thetis after the death of Patroclus—Achilles
is unable to reconcile his inner and outer hearing. In
Book 9, in his response to Phoenix, the emotions en-
gendered by the inner ear are displaced into belligerent
denunciation and belligerent generosity:

> "It does not become you
> to love this man, for fear you turn hateful to me, who
> love you.
> It should be your pride with me to hurt whoever shall
> hurt me.
> Be king equally with me; take half of my honour." (9.
> 613–16)

Let Phoenix stay with him in his tent, Achilles concludes, while Odysseus and Ajax take back his message
to the Achaeans. And then, almost parenthetically, he
makes his first concession: that only next day will "we"
decide whether to go home or to remain at Troy. Like
the speech that it concludes, the concession is a half-
conscious response to what Achilles has half understood.

iii

In the supplications of Meleager that mirror those of
Achilles, the successive suppliants are the Aetolian elders,
Meleager's parents and sisters, and his personal friends.

On the surface, this is a puzzling pattern, and all the more puzzling when it is recapitulated in the macrocosm of Book 9. By character and choice, Odysseus is in the fullest sense a delegate of the Achaeans and of Agamemnon, a man in whom the diplomat has superseded a direct and simpler self. Phoenix represents, as we have seen, a symbolic and hermaphroditic parent. And Ajax represents, in his simple and soldierly way, the values of comradeliness and friendship. Yet the movement through the three supplications is clearly meant to be an escalation, since in each case a fourth suppliant waits in the wings, the most important of all: Cleopatra in the parable of Meleager and Patroclus in the macrocosm of Book 9.

In what way can a friend be said to be superior to a parent in the intensity of his appeal? Superficially the statement is preposterous in a poem obsessively concerned with parents and children, with parenthood in both its literal and symbolic capacities.

An answer is possible only when we take account of an element in Homer that even now we have barely touched on. It is the vision of a post-heroic society and its moral foundations; specifically, a vision of the *polis*.

That the *Iliad* is concerned with a city, indeed that it takes its conventional name from one, is hardly a fact of which the world could lose sight. As long as it was felt to be essentially a Mycenaean poem, the separation between Troy and the *polis* of classical times was obviously complete. The monarchy of Priam, Asiatic and polygamous, could scarcely have anything in common with the democracy of Pericles.

Yet Troy (with its monarchical reflection in Calydon) is not the only city in the poem. Two more appear in Book 18, on the shield of Achilles, a city at peace and a city at war, both nameless, and they are juxtaposed with a clarity that verges on the allegorical. In the city at peace, the joys and benefits of peace are summed in marriages and festivals. The city at war resembles Troy, though not precisely, and the account of the warfare between its defenders and attackers ends inconclusively, *in medias res*, as if the slaughter will go on forever.

Yet the city at peace contains a germ of war. Even as the marriage dances are underway,

The people were assembled in the market place, where a quarrel
had arisen, and two men were disputing over the blood price
for a man who had been killed. One man promised full restitution
in a public statement, but the other refused and would accept nothing.
Both then made for an arbitrator, to have a decision;
and people were speaking up on either side, to help both men.
But the heralds kept the people in hand, as meanwhile the elders
were in session on benches of polished stone in the sacred circle
and held in their hands the staves of the heralds who lift their voices.
The two men rushed before these, and took turns speaking their cases,
and between them lay on the ground two talents of gold, to be given
to that judge who in this case spoke the straightest opinion.
But around the other city were lying two forces of armed men. . . . (18.497–509)

The scene on the shield has nothing to do with the
Mycenaeans, any more than the third play of the *Oresteia*
describes the judicial procedures of Athens in 1400 B.C.
It represents the *polis*, and specifically the Athenian *polis*,
as we know it in the archaic and classical periods, and
it identifies the moral heart of that *polis* as the settlement
of blood disputes by arbitration, the imposition of a secular and substitutive justice for the primitive heroic code
of vengeance.

The older style of Homeric criticism would be quick
to identify such a passage as a late interpolation. One
ought to be prepared to agree, provided the door is left
open to one possibility: that the "interpolator" of the
cities on the shield, and perhaps of the shield as a whole,
and perhaps of the supplication of Phoenix, and perhaps
of the *Doloneia,* is perhaps the author/editor of the *Iliad*
as a whole. Even Book 24, after all, has been designated
by some scholars as a late addition. Interpolation on
such a scale, and the possible omission of materials forever lost, is creation.

What we see on the shield of Achilles tells us that a
city at peace is the highest development of humanity,
and that it is purchased at the price of the magnificent
heroism we have seen in the first third of the poem. Men
can outgrow the heroic only by making themselves
smaller; and the act of will by which they do this is the
ultimate heroism.

In its insistent emphasis on relationships that transcend
the ties of blood, and particularly in the supplication of
Phoenix in Book 9, the *Iliad* prepares us for what we see
on the shield of Achilles and for the terrible irony that
it is the very shield he carries in his murderous heroic
rampage against the Trojans. It would be absurd to

suggest that a *polis* was ever held together by emotions like those Phoenix feels for Achilles or Achilles for Patroclus. But those emotions provide a kind of crystalline evidence for the transcendence of blood, especially when we note how they play off dialectically against the blood history of those involved: Phoenix cursed by the chthonic powers for whom blood and vengeance is the very function of existence, Patroclus a refugee from a system of value that must avenge even an accidental slaying by a child with the life of the slayer.

In Book 9, the chthonic is insistently played off against the bloodless, the absolute against the reasonably human, pity against pitilessness, social bonds against heroic self-containment. Phoenix offers the argument that "thus it was in the old days also, the deeds that we hear of/from the great men, when the swelling anger descended upon them./The heroes would take gifts; they would listen, and be persuaded." Even the parable thus introduced contradicts the generalization: Meleager's behavior indicates how opposed to persuasion and compromise is the heroic code. It is precisely a post-heroic and civic morality that Phoenix is trying to bolster, and of all the heroes in the *Iliad* only Hector in his comparative fragility, and in the effort of will that his role requires, approaches it.

But it is Ajax whose supplication, the briefest of the three, offers us the most compressed and lucid vision of the post-heroic order. Ajax is neither a subtle diplomat nor a symbolic parent; his relationship to Achilles falls somewhere between the antipodes of manipulation and passionate closeness. And he offers Achilles in rapid succession four grounds for altering his stand, each of which emphasizes the voluntary submission of the individual to an order outside of himself:

"it is best to go back quickly
and tell this story, though it is not good, to the Danaans
who sit there waiting for us to come back, seeing that
    Achilles
has made savage the proud-hearted spirit within his body.
He is hard, [1] and does not remember that friends' af-
    fection
wherein we honoured him by the ships, far beyond all
    others.
Pitiless. [2] And yet a man takes from his brother's slayer
the blood price, or the price for a child who was killed,
    and the guilty
one, when he has largely repaid, stays still in the country,
and the injured man's heart is curbed, and his pride, and
    his anger
when he has taken the price; but the gods put in your
    breast a spirit
not to be placated, bad, for the sake of one single
girl. [3] Yet now we offer you seven, surpassingly lovely,
and much besides these. Now make gracious the spirit
    within you.
[4] Respect your own house; see, we are under the same
    roof with you,
from the multitude of the Danaans, we who desire beyond
    all
others to have your honour and love, out of all the Acha-
    ians." (9.626–43)

Ajax's plea recapitulates in powerful miniature the
supplications that have preceded his own, and transforms
them in the process. His opening plea, on the grounds of
heroic friendship, is uniquely his own, the one that he is
most fitted to make as the exemplification of a stubborn,
secular loyalty and valor. His second plea anticipates
even more clearly than the speech of Phoenix the civic

morality that we will see at work on the shield of Achilles, and at the same time echoes the words of Phoenix and the experience of Patroclus. Meleager, we will remember, seems to have slain his mother's brother; Patroclus, as his ghost reminds Achilles in Book 23, "killed the son of Amphidamas. I was/a child only, nor intended it, but was angered over a dice game." Ajax's third plea recapitulates the supplication of Odysseus. And the fourth sums up the crucial voluntarism of hospitality, the hospitality that he has shown the suppliants when they first arrived at his tent, the hospitality that he will show to Priam in Book 24, the hospitality whose granting or violation is the central concern of the *Odyssey*.

Of the four pleas of Ajax, none can be connected explicitly with the archaic and classical *polis*. Yet each offers a mode of human connection analogous to it. Friendship, the substitution of monetary payment for the *lex talionis*, the acceptance of surrogate compensation, and the tendering of hospitality to the man who enters one's house even when he is an unconnected stranger—the four together make up a state of mind, the sensibility of a postheroic universe. In this sense the appeal of Ajax, and not that of Phoenix, represents the climactic supplication of Book 9, and the one that finally wrings a concession from Achilles. The concession is inadequate and the *Iliad* is a tragedy. Book 9 ends with a bitter repudiation of Achilles by the warrior who most exemplifies the heroic code, Diomedes, breaker of horses.

6
THE KILLING OF LYKAON

i

The death of Patroclus stands halfway between Book 9 and Book 24. Book 9 points toward it, Book 24 derives from it; it is the point of focus through which we must pass as we move with Achilles from a heroic to a post-heroic world.

The death of heroism is preceded by its hypertrophy. The first third of the *Iliad* offers us heroics that are high-hearted and uncomplicated, epitomized in the exploits of Diomedes. After Book 9, as the pace and violence of the fighting escalates, it is the shout of Hate that sums up the tone of the poem. Dolon is the first of many Trojan suppliants to be killed in the act of pleading for mercy. Early in Book 11, Agamemnon kills two sons of Priam, Isus and Antiphus, and goes on to kill the supplicating sons of the Trojan Antimachus. As the first of these dual killings is underway, Homer glances at the customs of combat that once obtained in the war and that now have passed forever from an increasingly savage scene. Achilles had caught Isus and Antiphus "at the knees of Ida, and bound them in pliant/willows as they watched by their sheep, and released them for ransom."

Before the death of Patroclus, all the combatants are involved in an escalating slaughter whose motifs are a brutal vaunting before and after the killing of one's enemy, refusal of supplications for mercy, and, insistently, the slaying of kin: of brothers and blood relatives together, and of warriors whose family ties are carefully cited in the narrative. When Achilles returns to the battle after the death of his companion, it is he who carries on this slaughter and these motifs.

This is the famous *aristeia* of Achilles, the moment in the poem and in his life when he attains the apex of his career and kills, climactically, his greatest enemy. In his murderous rampage against the Trojans, Achilles is insistently compared to fire, perhaps the least subtle of the elements, and almost the last quality we would look for in the narrative is a subtlety worthy of comparison with Book 9.

Yet the subtlety of the *aristeia* exceeds every comparable achievement in the poem, and perhaps anything comparable in the literature of the world. It is infused with paradox on a gargantuan scale; before our eyes, simultaneously and inextricably, its protagonist attains both the apex and the nadir of being, the strength of a superhuman force and the weakness of a child, the utter assured self-possession of a warrior in his function and an abrasive hideousness that affronts and provokes the very nature of the universe.

The subtlety of the *aristeia* is achieved through patterning, the kind of patterning that we have already seen in Apuleius and that is the peculiar genius of literature in the oral and rhetorical tradition. But the patterning of the

Metamorphoses is a casual affair compared to what we find in the *aristeia,* where each stroke and movement of the narrative communicates to the reader the force, direction, and point of the Homeric intelligence.

ii

The paradox of Achilles is established on the very threshold of the *aristeia.* He must kill Hector, he tells his mother in Book 18, and she begins to cry:

"Then I must lose you soon, my child, by what you are
          saying,
since it is decreed your death must come soon after
          Hektor's."
     Then deeply disturbed Achilleus of the swift feet
          answered her:
"I must die soon, then; since I was not to stand by my
          companion
when he was killed." (18.95–99)

Achilles' reply is oblique to the real gist of what Thetis has said, in a way that recalls his reply to Phoenix. Thetis is mourning over him, as he has himself mourned Patroclus; he hears only the prophecy of his death. Since he knows of that prophecy already, the "deep disturbance" he feels may indicate that he has caught, and yet not understood, the deeper tones of his mother's speech. At any rate the Greek text drives home the cross-purposes of the dialogue by not succumbing to anything like Lattimore's easy parallel of "lose you soon" and "die soon": "Then lost from me, child, you must be," would be a closer approximation of Thetis' opening words, while the crisp compression of his reply is *autika tethnaien,* a rhetoric utterly at odds with the caesurae of her grief.

The remainder of Achilles' speech drives his paradox home. Achilles wishes "that strife would vanish away from among gods and mortals,/and gall, which makes a man grow angry for all his great mind," and he resolves to beat down his anger toward Agamemnon. Yet he can reiterate with no irony his resolution to kill Hector, and he concludes:

> "Now I must win excellent glory,
> and drive some one of the women of Troy, or some
>   deep-girdled
> Dardanian woman, lifting up to her soft cheeks both
>   hands,
> to wipe away the close bursts of tears in her lamentation."
> (18.121–24)

The very man whose mother is weeping over him, and who has risen to a philosophic sense of strife and anger as the enduring curse of human life, can exult at the prospect of making Trojan women weep for their sons and husbands! The sense of Achilles conveyed here is that of a sensibility that has immeasurably widened itself since Book 1, but whose inner integration cannot keep pace with the growth it is undergoing. There is a gap of understanding within this man, a circuit that has failed to close. The violent anger that he will soon turn against the Trojans can be compared to the sparks that seek to close what is doomed to stay open: it is a desperate and ultimately false solution to the problem, and its violence is proportionate to its failure.

The state of mind revealed in the dialogue with Thetis prepares us for the symbolic function—or functions—of

Achilles' armor. Here the dialectic of the *Iliad* rises to a vibrant and startling intensity. Thetis, the least pugnacious divinity in the poem and the one in whom maternal compassion has swallowed up every other quality, is also the one who is forced to supplicate Hephaestus for the armor, the very means by which her son will bring death and mourning to the Trojans. Hephaestus, himself a pathetic antithesis to heroism, grants her supplication, because, when his own mother repudiated him for his lameness, Thetis and her sister Eurynome assumed a symbolic motherhood over him. The artwork of Hephaestus is that of peace rather than war: in the nine years that Thetis and Eurynome protected him, he made pins and clasps, cups and necklaces. The armor he makes is strangely unwarlike and he himself refers to it as something to look at rather than something to fear. On the shield he portrays the entire order of a functioning and harmonious universe, and an explicit allegory of the blessings of peace and civic rather than heroic order; and this is the armor that Achilles will wear in mercilessly slaughtering the Trojans. When the formal battle resumes in Book 20, and gods as well as men take their positions against each other, the enemy of Hephaestus is "the great deep-eddying river/who is called Xanthos by the gods, but by mortals Skamandros." It is fire against water, the divinity responsible for Achilles' armor against the one whose role it will be to establish Achilles' paradoxical weakness. Opposed as they are in the battle, Hephaestus and Scamander have something profoundly in common. Neither is warlike by nature, both are forces more provoked than provoking, both belong to the order of the shield rather than the order of the rampant Achilles. Even when Hephaestus defeats the river and allows the *aristeia* to pursue its course, it will be because he is supplicated by his mother and not because he has come to share the values of the man who wears his armor.

iii

In Books 20 and 21, after the onset of the battle and the *aristeia,* there are six major encounters or scenes. They could be called themes and variations since they echo each other with an extraordinary density, a steady yet modulated interweaving of characters and motifs, which at the same time draws into itself the macrocosm of the poem. In the first of these, Apollo disguises himself as the Trojan warrior Lykaon, and advises Aeneas not to en-counter Achilles. In the second, Aeneas does encounter Achilles and is rescued from almost certain death by Poseidon, who sweeps a mist across the eyes of Achilles. The third is a combat between Achilles and Hector, in which Apollo rescues Hector by wrapping him in mist. In the fourth, Achilles captures Lykaon himself, and kills him, flinging his body into the river Scamander, which he has already defiled with slaughtered Trojans. The fifth is a combat between Achilles and the disconcerting Trojan warrior Asteropaeus, an ambidextrous fighter who is the grandson of a river and who succeeds—uniquely in the *Iliad*—in wounding Achilles. Finally Achilles en-counters the river Scamander himself, and flees from his onrush in terror, to be rescued momentarily by Athene and Poseidon and finally by Hera and Hephaestus. The six encounters are followed by a half-farcical scene on Olympus and the rescue of the Trojan Agenor from Achilles in a mist; and the narrative moves rapidly thereafter to the final combat and death of Hector, the subject of Book 22.

Even in bare paraphrase it is clear that the patterning of the *aristeia* fuses repetition and contrast, analogy and alternation. Achilles is uniformly successful against his human antagonists—at least, he is uniformly undefeated—and yet undergoes some remarkable ups-and-downs. The incomparable strength that makes it necessary for the gods to rescue some of his opponents, and for the remainder to die, is followed by his total helplessness before the enraged Scamander, which is followed in turn by his successful combat with Hector, the climactic battle of the *Iliad*. If strength brackets weakness, weakness nevertheless enters a disturbing note into what is often represented as an apotheosis of strength.

But bare paraphrase can only suggest the dialectical character of the *aristeia*. It is when we look more closely at the successive encounters that the Homeric achievement reveals its lucid complexity.

The opening encounters, of Apollo in disguise with Aeneas, and of Aeneas with Achilles, establish a series of strongly marked contrasts. Apollo, the god who has brought about Patroclus' death by striking him senseless from behind, bamboozles Aeneas into an encounter that means almost certain death for him, and does it on the ground that Aeneas is superior in birth to his opponent and will therefore be superior on the battlefield. His actions remind us of the terrible vulnerability of human beings in the face of the Olympians—Athene will fool Hector in precisely the same way—and they contrast remarkably with those of Poseidon, a bitter partisan of the Achaeans who nevertheless saves Aeneas from death because he is guiltless, because he is pious, and because the

Trojans are destined, through Aeneas, to survive the fall
of their city. The inversions are as fascinating here as
in the parable of Meleager. Just as Poseidon switches
sides, momentarily, for the best of reasons, so the god
who doomed Patroclus turns on the Trojan Aeneas in a
manner that suggests an underlying maliciousness, since
he knows as well as Hera and Poseidon that Aeneas could
never survive the combat. The *de facto* ally of Achilles,
otherwise his enemy, symbolizes the very divisiveness of
what is going on in Achilles himself. Poseidon's pity, and
the prophecy of Trojan endurance beyond the tragedy of
Troy, suggests the presence in the *aristeia* of a principle
that extends far beyond the apotheosis of strength that
it portrays.

Two orders are being invoked, and the contrast between them is established in the dialogue of Aeneas and
Achilles. Achilles is boastful and insulting. He wonders
whether Aeneas aspires to be lord of the Trojans, and
whether he has been promised a reward for killing him.
And he reminds Aeneas of how once

> "I caught you
> alone, and chased you in the speed of your feet down the
>   hills of Ida
> headlong, and that time as you ran you did not turn to
>   look back.
> Then you got away into Lyrnessos, but I went after you
> and stormed that place, with the help of Athene and of
>   Zeus father,
> and took the day of liberty away from their women
> and led them as spoil, but Zeus and the other gods saved
>   you.
> I think they will not save you now . . ." (20.188–95)

The motif of chaser and chased is central to the *aristeia*

and has its brilliant ironic inversion when Achilles becomes the Chaser Chased, fleeing on his swift feet from
the wrath of Scamander. Eventually Achilles will chase
Hector three-and-a-half times around the walls of Troy,
but only after he has undergone a humiliation that puts
that event into a perspective simultaneously tragic and
satiric. And something of this complex bracketing is already suggested when Aeneas replies to Achilles' surly
and sadistic challenge with a supremely adequate and
dignified speech. He begins by talking about his own
and Achilles' parents and at first one might expect that
he will repeat Apollo's derogation of Achilles as a genea-
logical inferior. Instead, he goes out of his way to be re-
spectful to his opponent's parents; his concern is "that
of these parents/one group or the other will have a dear
son to mourn for/this day." Then he goes on to rehearse
his genealogy in more detail, in such a way as to make it
clear that he, through his forebears, cannot be separated
from the history of Troy, that as a descendant of Dardanus, Erichtonius, and Tros he as much as Hector is
Troy incarnate.

Then Aeneas casts his spear at Achilles. The potent
counterforce that he represents in the *aristeia* of his opponent is summed up symbolically when Achilles thrusts
his shield out in fright. The voice of Homer exclaims
nepios—"Fool!"—and criticizes Achilles' incomprehension
that "the glorious gifts of the gods are not easily broken/
by mortal men," but when the spear hits the chield it
pierces two of its five layers. Aeneas' potency appears
again in the huge rock that he is able to heave in self-
defense, and with no god helping. It comes out finally in
the reason that Poseidon gives for rescuing him, that
"Dardanos was nearest to Kronides [Zeus] of all his sons
that have been born to him from mortal women." It is

not only Poseidon's pity that goes into action against
Achilles, but Zeus' love for Aeneas' ancestor, and the
effect of that love on Poseidon's affection for his brother
—the same brother he elsewhere rebels against in his desire to bring glory to the Achaeans! It is as if Achilles had
suddenly run into a wall compounded of all the values he
has not yet attained. Aeneas, who subsumes Troy within
his ancestry and his destiny, is Achilles' anti-self: their
fortunes as well as their temperaments are studies in contrast. The point is driven home when Poseidon warns
Aeneas against trying to do battle with Achilles again;
when the latter is dead, then "there shall be no other
Achaian able to kill you."

Just as Achilles could offer Aeneas only a surly and
spiteful challenge, and received in reply a speech whose
beauty and dignity are striking, so he offers after the
salvation of Aeneas a comment whose resentful stupefac-
tion contrasts dramatically with what has provoked it:

"Can this be? Here is a strange thing I see with my own
    eyes.
Here is my spear lying on the ground, but I can no longer
see the man, whom I was charging in fury to kill him.
Aineas was then one beloved of the immortal
gods. I thought what he said was ineffectual boasting.
Let him go. He will not again have daring to try me
in battle, since even now he was glad to escape my onset."
                                                    (20.344–50)

iv

In the events that follow the encounter with Aeneas,
the implications of that encounter are echoed and reinforced. It is a process that extends down to the minute

details of the narrative, yet with no loss of narrative conviction and no sense of a mechanistic or artificial scheme being imposed on the reader.

In schematic form, those events are:

1. Apollo warns Hector not to fight Achilles alone.
2. Achilles kills Iphition, and vaunts over the body.
3. Achilles kills, in rapid succession, Demoleon and Hippodamas.
4. Achilles kills Polydorus, youngest and best-loved son of Priam, brother of Hector.
5. Hector tries to avenge his brother in combat with Achilles, and is rescued by Poseidon.
6. Achilles kills, in rapid succession, Dryops, Demouchus, and the brothers Dardanus and Laogonus.
7. Tros supplicates Achilles for mercy; Achilles kills him.
8. Achilles kills, in rapid succession, Moulius, Echeclus, Deucalion, Rhigmus, and Areithous.
9. The advance of Achilles, which concludes Book 20, is described in brilliant simile.
10. Book 21 begins with the slaughter of the Trojans in the waters of Scamander, on whose shores Achilles finds the unarmed Lykaon, whom he kills in spite of his supplication for mercy.

Of these ten events, numbers 3, 6 and 8 can be lumped together as formal interstices. With the exception of the significantly named Dardanus (whose significance is also enhanced by the fact that he is killed with a brother), the Trojans slain here are the Homeric equivalent of cannon fodder. Achilles is on the rampage and their deaths are intended simply and clearly to illustrate that fact. We are told almost nothing about them except the actual manner of their deaths.

Sometimes Homer tells us more and when this happens,

outside the formal interstices of slaughter, the content consistently frames or delimits the "space" of Achilles, reminding us of Aeneas and of the sensibility Achilles has not yet attained. The salvation of Hector by Apollo is a clear echo of the salvation of Aeneas. Achilles' vaunting over the body of Iphition recalls the combat with Aeneas and prepares us for the vaunting of Achilles over the bodies of Lykaon and Hector. The killing of Polydorus, whose ties of love to Priam are strongly emphasized, is an anticipation of the loss that will affect Priam the most: the death of Hector himself. And the killing of Trojans with names like Dardanus and Tros makes an obvious point. As he kills Dardanus, Tros, Lykaon, and Hector, Achilles is symbolically killing Troy. But we know already, from the combat with Aeneas, that Troy cannot be killed, that for all its vulnerability to his rage it is a principle that stands beyond him, a level of being that he cannot touch. The Romans were more than arbitrary in choosing Aeneas for an ancestor, and the Trojan sympathies of the Middle Ages stemmed from a remarkably sensitive understanding of Homer and Virgil.

Even as the "space" of Achilles is subtly bracketed, the slaughter of the Trojans worsens in intensity. They are now in full flight before Achilles: half stampede in terror toward the city, but are frustrated in their flight by Hera; half crowd into the waters of Scamander to escape their pursuer. Achilles leaps into the water and begins to slaughter them, spilling their blood into an element that we know is also a god. And when he is tired of killing, he chooses twelve of them to sacrifice on the pyre of Patroclus.

It is at this point that Achilles comes

upon a son of Dardanian Priam

as he escaped from the river, Lykaon, one whom he himself
had taken before and led him unwilling from his father's
      gardens
on a night foray. He with the sharp bronze was cutting
      young branches
when an unlooked-for evil thing came upon him, the
      brilliant
Achilleus, who that time sold him as a slave in strong-
      founded Lemnos
carrying him there by ship, and the son of Jason paid
      for him;
from there a guest and friend who paid a great price
      redeemed him,
Eetion of Imbros, and sent him to shining Arisbe;
and from there he fled away and came to the house of
      his father.
For eleven days he pleasured his heart with friends and
      family
after he got back from Lemnos, but on the twelfth day
      once again
the god cast him into the hands of Achilleus, who this time
was to send him down unwilling on his way to the
      death god. (21.34–48)

As usual this reaches out in a multitude of directions.
Achilles first captured Lykaon in a night foray, like
Diomedes' and Odysseus' coming upon Dolon. He came
upon him, however, in a pastoral scene, much as he once
came upon Aeneas tending cattle on Ida. He chased
Aeneas from place to place in a nightmare pursuit; Lykaon
was forced to go from place to place in a manner emphasized by that unexplained need, when he was already
a free man, to flee from Arisbe. As a son of Priam, Lykaon
sets up a pattern of echo and analogy with Aeneas, Polydorus, and Hector himself. (His familial bonds are emphasized by the very strangeness of his history.) Even the

fact that he meets his fate on the twelfth day after his return has a nearby echo in the twelve unlucky Trojans whom Achilles has just destined for human sacrifice, and a broader structural parallel in the twelve Thracians killed by Diomedes and Odysseus in Book 10.

But the full significance of Lykaon can only be understood when we are told that he is

naked and without helm or shield, and he had no spear left
but had thrown all these things on the ground, being weary and sweating
with the escape from the river, and his knees were beaten with weariness. . . . (21.50–52)

Lykaon is in fact very much in the position of a child, an ultimate dependent. If he is comparable to Dolon, who was pitifully helpless and childlike in the hands of Odysseus and Diomedes, he carries his helplessness still further: for Dolon had, at any rate, a wolf's pelt on his back, a cap, a spear, and a bow. And when Lykaon supplicates Achilles for life it is in terms that are worth looking at closely, terms that are used here and here alone:

Achilleus,
I am at your knees. Respect my position, have mercy upon me.
I am in the place, illustrious, of a suppliant who must be honoured,
for you were the first beside whom I tasted the yield of Demeter
on that day you captured me in the strong-laid garden
and took me away from my father and those near me, and sold me away into sacred Lemnos. . . . (21.73–79)

When Achilles had Lykaon in a position of helplessness once before, he committed an act which in Lykaon's curious and emphatic wording has a ritual force: he was the first after Priam to have Lykaon eat with him in the position of a child or dependent. In the first of the three lines I have italicized, Lattimore's metre puts the emphasis on "first," but the Greek is *par gar soi protoi pasamen Demeteros akten*, "for with YOU I first tasted Demeter's yield," and the emphasis is reinforced by the easy rhyme of the opening monosyllables.

Food-giving is the very center of hospitality, and hospitality is sacred because in its food-giving aspect it bridges the worlds of personal and social life. One owes to a guest what one owes to one's child. Achilles' hospitality is an emphatic part of his character: he extends it in exemplary fashion to the suppliants in Book 9 and to Priam in Book 24. And Phoenix, the house-guest of Peleus who becomes a father to the helpless child Achilles, is the living paradigm of this intersection. At the center of his relationship with Achilles is the fact that

> you would not go with another
> out to any feast, nor taste any food in your own halls
> until I had set you on my knees, and cut little pieces
> from the meat, and given you all you wished, and held the
> wine for you. (9.486–89)

Phoenix is a substitute father for Achilles, more intense in his relationship with him than Peleus could ever be. Achilles, who takes Lykaon "away from my father and those near me," becomes a curious inverted father too, for he must protect his captive if only to sell him. And both Phoenix and Lykaon hold up the sharing of food as a secred act that commits the giver to the recipient forever.

Certainly this helps to explain why, when Lykaon has invoked yet another parallel by stressing that Achilles has already killed his brother Polydorus, Priam's other child by the same mother, and that "I am not from the same womb as Hector"—a terrible appeal, this, within the framework of kinship that pervades the *Iliad*—why at this point Achilles speaks to Lykaon in terms that have always haunted the reader of the *Iliad:*

Poor fool, no longer speak to me of ransom, nor argue it.
In the time before Patroclus came to the day of his destiny
then it was the way of my heart's choice to be sparing
of the Trojans, and many I took alive and disposed of
    them.
Now there is not one who can escape death, if the gods
    send
him against my hands in front of Ilion, not one
of all the Trojans and beyond all others the children of
    Priam.
So, friend, you die also. Why all this clamour about it?
Patroclus also is dead, who was better by far than you are.
Do you not see what a man I am, how huge, how splendid
and born of a great father, and the mother who bore me
    immortal?
Yet even I have also my death and my strong destiny,
and there shall be a dawn or an afternoon or a noontime
when some man in the fighting will take the life from me
    also
either with a spearcast or an arrow flown from the
    bowstring. (21.99–113)

Achilles' speech is more than magnificent. It has an almost hypnotic fascination, and Lattimore has barely captured its supreme combination of affectionate address and the assertion of power, calmness, and menace. So measured and poised is the delivery, especially in the section beginning *alla, philos, thane kai su,* "So, friend, you die also," that it seems to come from a timeless universe quite removed from the battlefield, where Achilles can finally contemplate the fact of death without the restless frenzy that precedes and follows this scene. It is Lykaon who has provoked this extraordinary rhetoric, though the relationship of stimulus and response is as oblique as it was in the great dialogues between Achilles and Phoenix, Achilles and Thetis. When Achilles is supplicated in the name of life the appeal sinks deep but the reply comes from life's antithesis. His tone acknowledges the symbolic childhood of Lykaon even as he vows to slaughter the children of Priam. To move beyond good and evil in this way, to the point at which a man can acknowledge the thing he destroys, is the apotheosis of heroism. In the dialectical structure of the *aristeia,* the greatest masterpiece of reverberating irony in our literature, this is the point at which the pendulum carries us to the furthest bounds of the heroic code, the hypertrophy that brings an order to the brink of obsolescence.

Lykaon's response makes clear that he has understood this quality of finality. His "knees and the inward/heart went slack. He let go of the spear and sat back, spreading/wide both hands." He prepares to take his death from the spear, on his knees, in a manner that is again unmistakably childlike, offering himself to it frontally as if it were a gift. But the way in which he dies suggests already a new movement of the pendulum. The offer is refused as Achilles resorts to an oblique rather than a frontal weapon, and "drawing his sharp sword struck him/beside the neck at the collar-bone, and the double-edged sword/plunged full-length inside."

v

The killing of Lykaon stands midway between the deaths of Patroclus and Hector. In his helplessness, Lykaon echoes both figures: Patroclus stunned by the blow of Apollo and Hector deluded by Athene. The killing of Patroclus, proceeding relentlessly from Book 9, brings the death of Hector relentlessly in its train. But the point of the *Iliad* is that there is a level of being which transcends the relentless, the automatic, the heroic, that man is not fully man until his gestures cease to be those of a predictable force, until he acknowledges a force beyond him compounded of his own immensely difficult self-repression and the recognition of the wider commonalty of mankind. It is after the killing of Lykaon that the *Iliad* makes its point most triumphantly clear. Achilles flings the body of Lykaon into the river Scamander and vaunts over it in terms parallel to his exultation at keeping the body of Hector from kinfolk and burial, and expresses more strongly than ever the wish to kill *all* the fleeing Trojans as well as the conviction that their river will be unable to stop him. With the order of a living universe on his shield, an order that corresponds to the ultimate vision of the *Iliad,* he is the embodiment of entropy and death.

At last the universe responds. The river Scamander grows angry and wonders how to stop the slaughter. In a characteristic analogy and anticipation, the next opponent Achilles meets is the disconcerting Asteropaeus, grandson of a river, who wounds him. Then, in a further check, Achilles has difficulty in killing him. His spear misses Asteropaeus (as it missed Aeneas) and embeds itself in the river bank. Three times Asteropaeus tries to

wrench it loose; as he pulls at it a fourth time Achilles
kills him, as Hector will be killed in his fourth circuit
around the walls of Troy. Achilles vaunts over him in
terms that echo Apollo's incitement of Aeneas, terms that
mock Asteropaeus' ancestry and boast of his own genea-
logical superiority. No river is the equal of Zeus, he in-
sists, and not the Ocean itself, since "even Ocean is afraid
of the lightning of great Zeus/and the dangerous thunder-
bolt when it breaks from the sky crashing." (21.198–99)
In a remarkable leap the narrative and dramatic portions
of the poem fuse. Again and again the narrative voice of
the poem has compared Achilles to fire, and by speaking
of him in this way, from the "outside," has borne witness
to his heroic stature at the very time that he was derogat-
ing himself for being in his tent while Patroclus was dying.
Now, at the summit of his self-magnification, it is Achilles
who makes the same judgment and thus gives it a different gloss: from an excited simile striving to capture a
larger truth it becomes a swollen and hubristic challenge.
Superficially, his vaunt resembles the self-portrait he gave
Lykaon. But there Achilles achieved a remarkably dis-
passionate and aesthetic vision of his own greatness; part
of its miraculous poise is that it is somehow "inside" and
"outside" at the same time. Here, in his speech over
Asteropaeus, the balance is upset, and the very strength
he lauds is not his own but his great-grandfather's.

In the combat with Asteropaeus, Achilles has symbolically wounded the shore of Scamander with his spear, and
when he abandons the corpse its symbolic unity with the
river is clear: Asteropaeus lies "sprawled in the sands and
drenched in the dark water." A series of further killings
follows, quick and perfunctory; the river, irritated and yet
still polite, asks that he stop congesting it with corpses,

and reproaches Apollo for not protecting the Trojans; and Achilles, who only a moment before had promised Scamander to keep clear of him, abruptly—in a final fit of hubris—leaps into his waters to continue the slaughter.

There is no need to rehearse the famous and nightmarish pursuit of Achilles by Scamander, which echoes so many similar actions in the *Iliad* but most of all the chase of Hector around the walls of Troy. What is worth noting is the precise language of the appeal that Achilles makes to the great-grandfather of whose protection and power he has so recently been boasting:

"Father Zeus, no god could endure to save me from the river
who am so pitiful. And what then shall become of me?
It is not so much any other Uranian god who has done this
but my own mother who beguiled me with falsehoods, who told me
that underneath the battlements of the armoured Trojans
I would be destroyed by the flying shafts of Apollo.
I wish now Hektor had killed me, the greatest man grown in this place.
A brave man would have been the slayer, as the slain was a brave man.
But now this is a dismal death I am doomed to be caught in,
trapped in a big river as if I were a boy and a swineherd
swept away by a torrent when he tries to cross in a rainstorm." (21.273–83)

To the consummate irony of the opening sentence, spoken as it is by the pitiless Achilles, there is only one comparable moment in the poem: the scene in which the wrathful Achilles sends Patroclus into battle and counsels him to self-restraint. But the sublimity of the irony in this passage has two further aspects. Achilles accuses of treachery the very mother whose full love for him he cannot understand, and who of all the deities in the *Iliad* seems furthest from the possibility of treachery. And in his peril and fear, his sudden reduction to helplessness, he compares himself to a child, a little boy.

In the "eye" of the poem, that is precisely what he becomes. Though Zeus seems not to be interested in saving the man who has boasted of his kinship, Poseidon and Athene "swiftly came near him/and stood beside him with their shapes in the likeness of mortals/and caught him hand by hand and spoke to him in assurance." Male and female the divinities come to the rescue, and the tableau they set up with Achilles is that of a child with its parents. They are bad parents, however, practicing the "beguilements" of which he accuses Thetis, for after a few words of reassurance they go away and leave him to the continuing, indeed the worsening, nightmare of the wrath of Scamander. The river intends to

"whelm his own body
deep, and pile it over with abundance of sands and rubble numberless, nor shall the Achaians know where to look for his bones to gather them, such ruin will I pile over him. And there shall his monument be made, and he will have
        no need
of any funeral mound to be buried in by the Achaians."
(21.318–23)

The river wants to frustrate the mourning for Achilles as badly as Achilles desires, in the slayings of Lykaon and Hector, to frustrate the mourning of Priam and the Trojans. Scamander's spectacular assault, and his reduction of Achilles to childish helplessness, is the most certain proof that such a desire is a negation and perversion of what Achilles will learn to see (in both senses of the adjective) as common humanity.

Achilles' bitterly unjust accusation of Thetis echoes on in the work. When he has escaped the river and before he finally encounters Hector he is beguiled again, not by Thetis but by Apollo, as Hector in turn is beguiled to his death by Athene, until it is only Achilles' anger, the mist over his eyes, that keeps him from seeing the obvious: that he is joined to his enemies in a world where only the immortals are free from death.

7
AFTER DIONYSUS

It is easy for us to believe that irony and action are antitheses in human experience. Recent writers have noted the preference of the rebellious young for sentimentality over irony, and their tendency to associate the latter with that most contemptible of oppressors, the college professor, the man who sees three sides to every question and no question worth fighting for.

In this way as in others they are children of the nineteenth century, whose most pervasive motif is the conception of consciousness as the curse of modernity and of action as the agency that enables the human mind to balance its accounts in favor of emotion and intuition. In *War and Peace*, the novel that seems almost a companion volume to the *Iliad*, Prince Andrew's character, bearing, and state of mind undergo an immense positive transformation through his involvement in war. It is a paradox that Tolstoy explores with Homeric thoroughness. But on its simplest level, strong or violent action as a cure for malaise of thought is a theme he shares with Tennyson and Matthew Arnold, Nechaev and Bakunin, Emerson and Rimbaud.

The climactic formulation of the idea is the Nietzschean
opposition of Apollo and Dionysus, and the related doctrines of the "Cambridge School" of anthropology. And
what we have to deal with at the present time is the
fact that the Nietzschean adversary posture, and the
specific doctrines associated with it, have themselves become conventional. In the novels of Mary Renault, the
influential criticism of Francis Fergusson, the Living Theater, and the metaphysics of the "New Reformation," the
assault conducted between 1870 and 1910 on the tradi-
tionalist bases of Western culture continues to live an
almost verbatim existence: continues to dissolve our texts
and artifacts ("Apollonian") into the ritual, blood, and
orgiastic irrationality of the "Dionysian."

An implication of Nietzsche and the Cambridge School
has come, in this way, to fulfillment. The text of a Greek
epic or tragedy may look pretty dull; but look behind it,
under it, and around it, and you will see the rite of can-
nibalism and slaughter of which it is the ethicalized echo
or dialectical manifestation. When Mary Renault sells the
Mycenaeans to her public by attributing to them a thrill-
ing—really quite African—irrationality, we can see the
comfortable way in which the world has taken Dionysus
to its heart. But Mary Renault, even at her best, is mar-
keted as an anodyne. It is when a college professor uses
a markedly Apollonian manner to convey the Dionysian
brutalities "underneath" a text that an intolerable mode
of irony makes its appearance, a tension only resolvable,
perhaps, by the apocalypse that will consume him.

It is Homer who carries us beyond the dialectic of
irony and commitment; and there is no better proof of
this than the dialectically opposed interpretations his text
has been put through. To violent ages he has been a phi-
losopher and an allegorist. To the age of triumphant ra-

tionalism, sick of its peace and civilization, he was barely distinguishable from his heroes, a bard chanting ancestral lays in a mead-hall. What is so hard to grasp is that he is two things simultaneously, a poet of transition who gives what is lost as well as what is gained its fullest possible development. Virgil pushes this characteristic a step further by infusing into the *Aeneid* a note of plangent regret for that which is inexorably left behind, the famous "Virgilian melancholy." But in Homer past and future are in perfect—which is to say, ironic—balance. We must leap from one to the other but there is really no halfway house between them, no aesthetic platform on which to indulge our regrets: the separation is as sharp as those other Homeric contrasts of life and death, night and day, fury and repose.

The birth of tragedy took place not in those proto-tragic satyr plays that flit through the pages of post-Nietzschean literary history, and that happen not to have existed,[25] but in the *Iliad* itself. And the *Iliad* seems to have arisen out of a moment of agonized social transition in Greek—probably Athenian—society, when the *polis* was brought to the brink of destruction by the war between "haves" and "have-nots."[26] The stylistic and structural breadth of Homer, the sheer inclusive capacity of the

25. Gerald Else's *The Origin and Early Form of Greek Tragedy* (Cambridge, Mass.: Harvard University Press, 1967), perhaps the most important classical study of the past decade, disposes in a hundred succinct pages of the Aristotelian and Nietzschean hypothesis that connects the origins of Attic tragedy with goats, satyrs, and the ecstatic worship of Dionysus.

26. On the Athenian social picture at the time that Solon instituted both the annual recitation of Homer and the poetic basis for Attic drama, see Else's book (*ibid.*). Else's argument lends indirect support to the possibility that the Homeric texts as we have them underwent a final and crucial compilation around the time of Solon and Pisistratus. This in turn would make it possible to speak of "our" Homer and the tragic drama derived from him as having undergone a nearly simultaneous birth.

Iliad, is no recurrent feature of primitive epic poetry: one looks for it in vain in *Beowulf* or the *Song of Roland.* It is the inclusiveness of an inclusive moment when the mind, with whatever pain, is stretched across alternative possibilities and manages through symbolism and fable to make sense of its experience. What Homer, Virgil, Apuleius, Shakespeare, and Tolstoy ultimately have in common is that they are the spokesmen for moments of this kind. With characteristic and life-giving irony they bring to simultaneous fulfillment the incompatible polarities of historical and personal experience. We read them with new eyes because our world is like theirs.

SELECTED BIBLIOGRAPHY

Apuleius. *The Golden Ass.* Translated by W. Adlington, revised by S. Gaselee. Cambridge, Mass.: Harvard University Press (Loeb Classical Library), 1965.

Apuleius. *The Golden Ass.* Translated by Jack Lindsay. Bloomington, Ind.: Indiana University Press (Midland paperback edition), 1962.

Apuleius. *Les Métamorphoses.* Edited by D. S. Robertson and Paul Vallette. 3 vols. Paris: Société d'édition "Les Belles Lettres," 1956.

Matthew Arnold. *On the Classical Tradition.* vol. 1 of *The Complete Prose Works of Matthew Arnold,* edited by R. H. Super. Ann Arbor: The University of Michigan Press, 1960.

Erich Auerbach. *Mimesis: The Representation of Reality in Western Literature.* New York: Doubleday Anchor Books, 1957.

Saint Augustine. *Confessions.* Translated by R. S. Pine-Coffin. Harmondsworth, Middlesex: Penguin Books, 1961.

Hans Baron. *The Crisis of the Early Italian Renaissance.* Princeton: Princeton University Press (rev. ed. 1-vol. paperback), 1966.

Thomas Carlyle. *The French Revolution: A History.* 3 vols. London: J. Fraser, 1837.

Charles Norris Cochrane. *Christianity and Classical Culture.* New York: Oxford University Press (Galaxy paperback ed), 1957.

Gerald Else. *The Origin and Early Form of Greek Tragedy.* Cambridge, Mass.: Harvard University Press, 1967.

Sigmund Freud. *Civilization and Its Discontents.* Translated by James Strachey. New York: W. W. Norton and Co. (college ed.), 1962.

Northrop Frye. "The Critical Path." *Daedalus* (Spring 1970).

Northrop Frye. *A Natural Perspective: The Development of Shakespearean Comedy and Romance.* New York: Harcourt, Brace and World (Harbinger paperback ed). 1965.

Genesis. Translated and edited by E. A. Speiser. New York: Doubleday and Co., 1964.

Siegfried Giedion. *Mechanization Takes Command: A Contribution to Anonymous History.* New York: Oxford University Press, 1948.

E. H. Gombrich. *Art and Illusion: A Study in the Psychology of Pictorial Representation.* 2nd ed. New York: Pantheon Books, 1965.

Paul Goodman. *The New Reformation: Notes of a Neolithic Conservative.* New York: Random House, 1970.

The Iliad of Homer. Translated by Richmond Lattimore. Chicago: University of Chicago Press (Phoenix paperback ed), 1951.

The Iliad of Homer. Edited by Walter Leaf and M. A. Bayfield. 2 vols. London: Macmillan and Co., 1895 and 1898.

Paul Junghanns. *Die Erzählungstechnik von Apuleius' Metamorphosen und Ihrer Vorlage.* Leipzig: Dieterich'sche Verlagsbuchhandlung, 1932.

Frank Kermonde. "On Shakespeare's Learning." Middletown, Conn.: Wesleyan University Center for Advanced Studies, 1965.

C. S. Lewis. *English Literature in the Sixteenth Century.* Oxford: Clarendon Press, 1954.

Adam Parry. "The Two Voices of Virgil's *Aeneid.*" *Arion 2* (Winter 1963).

Michael C. J. Putnam. *The Poetry of the "Aeneid": Four Studies in Imaginative Unity and Design.* Cambridge, Mass.: Harvard University Press, 1965.

D. W. Robertson, Jr. *A Preface to Chaucer: Studies in Medieval Perspective*. Princeton: Princeton University Press, 1962.

Joseph A. Russo. "Homer Against His Tradition." *Arion* 7 (Summer 1968).

Sir Ronald Syme. *The Roman Revolution*. Oxford: Clarendon Press, 1939.

Leo Tolstoy. *War and Peace*. Translated by Louise and Aylmer Maude. Oxford: Oxford University Press (World's Classics ed.), 1941.

Lynn White. *Medieval Technology and Social Change*. Oxford: Clarendon Press, 1962.

Cedric Whitman. *Homer and the Heroic Tradition*. Cambridge, Mass.: Harvard University Press, 1958.

Heinrich Wölfflin. *Renaissance and Baroque*. Translated by Kathrin Simon. Ithaca, N.Y.: Cornell University Press, 1966.

INDEX

135